Annie Martin

Home Life on an Ostrich Farm

Annie Martin

Home Life on an Ostrich Farm

ISBN/EAN: 9783337059033

Printed in Europe, USA, Canada, Australia, Japan

Cover: Foto ©ninafisch / pixelio.de

More available books at **www.hansebooks.com**

HOME LIFE

ON AN

OSTRICH FARM.

WITH TEN ILLUSTRATIONS.

BY

ANNIE MARTIN.

LONDON:
GEORGE PHILIP & SON, 32 FLEET STREET, E.C.
LIVERPOOL: 45 TO 51 SOUTH CASTLE STREET.
1890.

To T. M.

IN REMEMBRANCE OF OUR SOUTH AFRICAN LIFE.

PREFACE.

Some portions of the chapters on "Ostriches" and "Bobby" have already appeared, in an abridged form, in the *Saturday Review*. Part of the chapter on "The Climate of the Karroo" has also appeared in the *St. James's Gazette*.

By the kind permission of the editors of both papers I am now enabled to reprint these pages.

A. M.

CONTENTS.

CHAPTER I.
PORT ELIZABETH AND WALMER.

Early ambitions realized—Voyage to South Africa—Cape Town and Wynberg—Profusion of flowers—Port Elizabeth—Christmas decorations — Public library — Malays — Walmer — Hottentot huts — Our little house — Pretty gardens — Honey-suckers—Flowers of Walmer Common—Wax-creeper—Ixias—Scarlet heath—Natal lilies—"Upholstery flower"—Ticks—Commence ostrich-farming—Counting the birds—A ride after an ostrich   9

CHAPTER II.
SOME OF OUR PETS.

Friendliness of South African birds and beasts—Our secretary bird—Ungainly appearance of Jacob—His queer ways—Tragic fate of a kitten—A persecuted fowl—Our Dikkops—A baby buffalo—Wounded buffalo more dangerous than lion—A lucky stumble—Hunter attacked by "rogue" buffalo—A midnight ride—Followed by a lion—Toto—A pugnacious goose—South African climate dangerous to imported dogs—Toto and the crows—Animals offered by Moors in exchange for Toto   25

CHAPTER III.
PLANTS OF THE KARROO.

We move up-country—Situation of farm—Strange vegetation of Karroo district—*Karroo* plant—*Fei-bosch*—*Brack-bosch*—Our flowers—*Spekboom*—Bitter aloes—Thorny plants—*Wacht-een-Beetje*—Ostriches killed by prickly pear—Finger-poll—Wild tobacco fatal to ostriches—Carelessness of colonists—Euphorbias—Candle-bush   46

CHAPTER IV.
OUR LITTLE HOME.

Building operations—A plucking—Ugliness of Cape houses—Our rooms—Fountain in sitting-room a failure—Drowned pets—Decoration of rooms—Colonist must be Jack-of-all-trades—Cape waggons—Shooting expeditions—Strange tale told by Boer   61

CONTENTS.

CHAPTER V.

CLIMATE OF THE KARROO.

PAGE

Cape Colony much abused—Healthy climate—Wonderful cures of consumption—Karroo a good place for sanatorium—Rarity of illness and accidents—The young colonist—An independent infant—Long droughts—Hot winds—Dust storms—Dams—Advantage of possessing good wells—Partiality of thunderstorms—Delights of a brack roof—Washed out of bed—After the rain—Our horses—Effects of rain indoors—*Opslaag*—The Cape winter—What to wear on Karroo farms 72

CHAPTER VI.

OSTRICHES.

An unwilling ride—First sight of an ostrich farm—Ridiculous mistakes about ostriches—Decreased value of birds and feathers—Chicks—Plumage of ostriches—A frightened ostrich—The plucking-box—Sorting feathers—Voice of the ostrich—Savage birds—"Not afraid of a dicky-bird!"—Quelling an ostrich—Birds killed by men in self-defence—Nests—An undutiful hen—Darby and Joan—A disconsolate widower—A hen-pecked husband—Too much zeal—Jackie—Cooling the eggs—The white-necked crow—Poisoning jackals—Ostrich eggs in the kitchen—A quaint old writer on ostriches—A suppliant bird—Nest destroyed by enraged ostrich—An old bachelor ... 98

CHAPTER VII.

OSTRICHES (*continued*).

Vagaries of an incubator—Hatching the chicks—A bad egg—Human foster-mothers—Chicks difficult to rear—"Yellow-liver"—Cruel boys—Chicks herded by hen ostrich—Visit to Boer's house—A carriage full of ostriches—"The melancholy Jaques"—Ostriches at sea—A stampede—Runaway birds—Branding—Stupidity of ostriches—Accidents—Waltzing and fighting—Ostrich soup—An expensive quince—A feathered Tantalus—Strange things swallowed by ostriches—A court-martial—The ostrich, or the diamond?—A visit to the Zoo ... 130

CONTENTS.

CHAPTER VIII.
MEERKATS.

Meerkats plentiful in the Karroo—Their appearance—Intelligence—Fearlessness—Friendship for dogs—A meerkat in England—Meerkat an inveterate thief—An owl in Tangier—Taming full-grown meerkat—Tiny twins—A sad accident—Different characters of meerkats—The turkey-herd—Bob and the meerkat—" The Mouse " 157

CHAPTER IX.
BOBBY.

Bobby's babyhood—Insatiable appetite—Variety of noises made by Bobby—His tameness—Narrow escape from drowning—A warlike head-gear—Bobby the worse for drink—His love of mischief—He disarms his master—Meerkat persecuted by Bobby—Bobby takes to dishonest ways—He becomes a prisoner—His clever tricks—Death of Bobby 170

CHAPTER X.
OUR SERVANTS.

A retrospective vision—Phillis in her domain—Her destructiveness —Her ideas on personal adornment—The woes of a mistress— Eye-service—Abrupt departure of Phillis—Left in the lurch— Nancy and her successors—Cure of sham sickness—The thief's dose—Our ostrich-herd—A bride purchased with cows— English and natives at the Cape—Character of Zulus and Kaffirs 182

CHAPTER XI.
HOW WE FARED.

Angora goats—Difficulty of keeping meat—The plague of flies— Rations—Our store—Barter—Fowls—Chasing a dinner— Fowls difficult to rear—Secretary birds as guardians of the poultry-yard—Jacob in the Karroo—He comes down in the world—He dies—Antelopes—A springbok hunt—The Queen's birthday in the Karroo—Colonial dances—Our klipspringer— Superstition about hares—Game birds—*Paauw*—*Knorhaan*— Namaqua partridges—Porcupines—A short-lived pet—Indian corn—Stamped mealies—Whole-meal bread—Plant used for making bread rise—Substitutes for butter—*Priembesjes*—A useful tree—Wild honey—The honey-bird—Enemies of bees —Moth in bees' nests—Good coffee—Sour milk 203

CONTENTS.

CHAPTER XII.
KARROO BEASTS, BIRDS AND REPTILES.   PAGE

Leopard drowned in well—Baboons—Egyptian sacred animals on Cape farms—"Adonis"—A humiliating retreat—A baby baboon—Clever tricks performed by baboons—Adonis as a *Voorlooper*—A four-handed pointsman—Sarah—A baboon at the Diamond Fields—Adonis's shower-bath—His love of stimulants—His revengeful disposition—Pelops the dog-headed —Horus—*Aasvogels*—Goat-sucker—The butcher-bird's larder —Nest of the golden oriole—The kapok-bird—Snakes in houses—A puff-adder under a pillow—Puff-adder most dangerous of Cape snakes—Cobras—*Schaapsticker*—Ugly house-lizards—Dassie-adder—The dassie the coney of Scripture— Stung by a scorpion—Fight between tarantula and centipede —Destructive ants—The *Aardvaark*, or ant-bear—Ignominious flight of a sentry—Ant-lion—Walking-leaves—The Hottentot god—A mantis at a picnic 237

CHAPTER XIII.
OUR NEIGHBOURS.

Hospitality of Cape colonists—Cheating and jealousy in business — Comfortless homes — Spoilt children — Education — The "Schoolmaster"—Convent schools—A priest-ridden nation— The *Nachtmaal*—Old French names—A South African duke in Paris — Fine-looking men — Fat women — Ignorance of *Vrouws*—Boers unfriendly to English—A mean man 266

CHAPTER XIV.
GOOD-BYE.

Recalled to England—Regrets and farewells—Cape horses lacking in intelligence—"Old Martin"—A chapter of accidents—A horse "after Velasquez"—The Spy's revenge—Virtues and faults of Cape horses—Horse-sickness—Good-bye to Swaylands —Kaffir crane—The voyage home—Dogs in durance—St. Helena—A visit to Longwood—Home again 277

LIST OF ILLUSTRATIONS.

---o---

I.—Troop of Ostriches and Cart, with Prickly-Pear Leaves for food	*Frontispiece.*
II.—1. Jacob. 2. Toto	*Facing page* 26
III.—Some of the best kinds of Ostrich-bush:—1. Brack-bosch. 2. Ghanna. 3. Fei-bosch.	,, 48
IV.—Our Sitting-room	,, 66
V.—Ostriches in a Hot Wind	,, 80
VI.—Ostrich-chicks	,, 104
VII.—1. Ostrich-chick (Photographed from case in Stanley and African Exhibition)— 2. Ostriches meditating Escape through defective fence	,, 150
VIII.—A Meerkat	,, 158

HOME LIFE ON AN OSTRICH FARM.

CHAPTER I.

PORT ELIZABETH AND WALMER.

Early ambitions realized—Voyage to South Africa—Cape Town and Wynberg—Profusion of flowers—Port Elizabeth—Christmas decorations—Public library—Malays—Walmer—Hottentot huts—Our little house—Pretty gardens—Honey-suckers—Flowers of Walmer Common—Wax-creeper—Ixias—Scarlet heath—Natal lilies—"Upholstery flower"—Ticks—Commence ostrich-farming—Counting the birds—A ride after an ostrich.

In the year 1881, leaving our native land wrapped in the cold fogs of November, my husband and I started for South Africa; where it was the intention of the former to resume the occupation of ostrich-farming, engaged in which he had already spent many years in the Cape Colony. It was my first visit to South Africa, and I was looking forward with great pleasure to the realization of a very early wish; for the adventures of settlers in far-off lands had always from childhood been my favourite reading, and I had become firmly convinced that a colonial life would suit me better than any other. Nor have I been disappointed; but, looking back now on our life in South Africa, I can truthfully say that, though certainly lacking in adventure, it has—unlike many things long wished for and attained at last—in no way fallen short of my expectations.

The few hours we spent at Madeira were unfortunately during the night; and the beautiful island I was so longing to see remained hidden from view in a most tantalizing manner, without even the moonlight to give us some faint outline of its far-famed loveliness.

After a safe, but most uneventful voyage, enlivened by no more stirring incidents than the occasional breaking down of the engines, we at last looked up at the glories of Table Mountain, and came suddenly into summer; enjoying the flowers and bright sunshine of Cape Town all the more after the dreary weather we had left in England. We landed, and spent a few very pleasant days at the pretty suburb of Wynberg, from whence we took several beautiful drives. On one occasion we left the carriage, and walked over such a carpet of lovely and bright-coloured wild flowers as I have only once seen equalled, when riding some years before through Palestine and Syria. At the end of five minutes we stopped, and counted all the different sorts we had gathered, finding twenty-eight.

Another day we collected a number of leaves of the silver tree, which is found only on Table Mountain. The long, pointed leaves seem made of the glossiest pale-grey satin; you can write and paint on their soft surface, and numbers of them are for sale in the Cape Town shops, adorned with highly-coloured pictures of Table Mountain, steamers going at full speed, groups of flowers, Christmas good wishes, etc. We preferred, however, when enclosing the leaves in our letters home, to send them in all their native beauty, and with no clumsy human attempts at improvement.

The beautiful plumbago is one of the most common plants, and many of the hedges about Wynberg consist entirely of it; the masses of its delicate blue-grey flowers forming as graceful a setting for the pretty, neatly-kept gardens as can well be imagined.

We were quite sorry when the time came for going back to our steamer, Port Elizabeth being our destination. We landed there a few days before Christmas; and, soon after our arrival, walked out to Walmer to call on friends, whom we found busily engaged in decorating the little church. Their materials consisted simply of magnificent blue water-lilies—evidently the sacred blue lotus of the ancient Egyptians, with the sculptured representations of which they are identical —and large, pure white arums, or, as the colonists unromantically call them, "pig-lilies;" both being among the commonest of wild flowers about Walmer. These, with a few large fern-fronds, and the arum's own glossy leaves, formed the loveliest Christmas decoration I have ever seen.

There is not much to see in Port Elizabeth; indeed, it is rather uglier than the generality of colonial towns, built simply for business, and with no thought of the picturesque—and what few attempts at ornament have been made are rather disfiguring than otherwise. On a bare hill above the town there is a conspicuous monument, the builders of which appear to have been long undecided as to whether it should be a small pyramid or large obelisk; the result being an ugly compromise between the two. Another work of art, more nearly approaching the obelisk form, but equally far from the Egyptian model both in its shape and in the designs which decorate it, stands in the market-place, in front of the town hall. This latter was by far the best-looking building in Port Elizabeth, until, a few years ago, its appearance was completely spoilt by the addition of an ugly and ponderous clock-tower, quite out of proportion to the rest of the structure, which it seems threatening to crush with its overpowering size and weight. The interior of the town hall, however, compensates for its outward deficiencies; for it contains a most excellent public library, plentifully supplied with books of all kinds, newspapers, and magazines, in two comfortable and well-arranged rooms. It would be well indeed if England would take a lesson from the Cape Colony in this respect; for in all the smaller towns which we visited, *i.e.*, Cradock, Graaff-Reinet, Uitenhage, etc., we found good public libraries. There is a good club in Port Elizabeth, and several hotels, all of which we have tried at different times, finding the Standard (Main Street), though small and of unpretending exterior, by far the most comfortable. A little way out of the town there is a very good botanical garden, with a large conservatory, containing many beautiful palms, tree-ferns, and other tropical plants.

The Malays are the most picturesque feature of Port Elizabeth; and their bright-coloured Eastern dresses, and the monotonous chant of the priest announcing the hours of prayer from the minaret of the mosque, form a pleasing contrast to the surrounding everyday sights and sounds. Like most other Orientals, they are perfect artists in their appreciation of colour; and, fortunately, they are still old-fashioned enough not yet to have adopted the hideous coal-tar dyes with which Europe has demoralized the taste of some of their brethren in Cairo and Algiers. On Fridays, when all are wearing their best, you often see the most beautiful materials, and the loveliest combinations of colour; especially in the flowing robes of the priests, the tints of which always harmonize perfectly. Thus, for instance, you will see an outer garment of turquoise blue, worn over an inner one of "old gold;" delicate salmon colour over soft creamy white; rich orange in combination with the deepest maroon; with an infinite variety of other lovely tints, any of which a painter might covet for his studio. The Malays often wear as turbans some of the beautiful *sarongs* of Java, which are simply ordinary calico, painted by hand with a few good colours, and in the most artistic designs; of course there are never two alike, and in these days of machine-made sameness they are refreshing to behold. Some of the men wear immense hats, made of palm leaves very firmly and solidly plaited, and tapering to a point; they are made to fit the head by means of a small crown fixed inside, very like that of a college cap.

The Malay women, instead of gliding about veiled to the eyes, like their Mohammedan sisters in other parts of the world, wear the quaint costume which was the fashion among the Dutch women at the time when the Malay race first came as slaves to the Cape. The waist of the dress is extremely short; and the long and voluminous skirts, of which an infinite number seem to be worn, commence close under the arms, spreading out, stiffly starched and spotlessly clean, to dimensions rivalling those of the old hooped petticoats. The good-natured brown faces are most unbecomingly framed by bright-coloured silk handkerchiefs tightly bound under the chin, somewhat after the fashion of the Algerian Jewesses—giving the wearers an appearance of perpetual toothache. Many of the women wear noisy wooden clogs; kept from parting company with the bare feet by nothing but a kind of large button, curiously ornamented, projecting between the two first toes.

In the early days of slavery, when the Malays were brought up in the Dutch families, nearly all were Christians; and even so recently as when Sir Bartle Frere was governor there were comparatively few among them who could read the Koran. During the last few years, however, Mohammedanism has been rapidly gaining ground everywhere—the great university of El Azhar in Cairo, especially, training thousands of students to go out as emissaries into all parts of the East to make converts—and the Malays, in constantly increasing numbers, are embracing the creed of Islam. Many of them now save up their money for the pilgrimage to Mecca, which is their great ambition. They are very ignorant; and their Mohammedan fatalism, prejudicing them against all sanitary precautions—especially vaccination—adds very much to the difficulty of contending with small-pox and other epidemics when they appear. In 1882, when there was so severe an outbreak of small-pox in Cape Town and other parts of the colony, the Malays not only opposed all attempts made by the authorities to isolate cases, but did all in their power to spread the disease; many of them being found throwing infected clothing into houses.

After staying about a week in the town, we went out to live at Walmer, which is by far the pleasantest part of all the surroundings of Port Elizabeth, and which deserves to be more generally chosen as a residence by the wealthier inhabitants. It stands high, in a most healthy situation, and full in the path of that rough but benevolent south-east wind, which, owing to its kindly property of sweeping away the germs of disease, is called "the Cape doctor." Away beyond Walmer stretch miles of undulating common, covered with short bush and numberless varieties of wild flowers; and a breezy walk across part of this same common leads to Port Elizabeth. The walk is rather a long one; and often, before the arrival of our little "spider" from America, it would have been a comfort, after a long day in town, to avail ourselves of one of the numerous hired carriages for the return journey, were not the drivers of these vehicles so exorbitant in their charges as almost to rival those of New York. They demand ten shillings for the drive to Walmer, taking the passenger only one way; and this too often in a vehicle so near the last stage of dilapidation as to suggest fears of the final collapse occurring on the road. The importunity of the drivers is most troublesome; and when, in spite of their efforts, you remain obdurate, and they fail to secure you as a "fare," they do their best to run over you, hoping no doubt that they may thus at least have a chance of driving you to the hospital. Their cab-stand, where, like a row of vultures, they sit waiting for their prey, is on the market-place; and as you cross the latter, bound for the reading-room, with ears deaf to their shouts, and eyes resolutely fixed on the door of the town hall, leaving no doubt as to your intention *not* to take a drive, the whole rank move forward in a simultaneous charge; pursuing and surrounding you with artful strategic movements and demoniac cries, and with so evident an intention to knock you down if possible, that when at last you stand safe on the town hall steps, you realize the feelings of Tam O'Shanter on gaining "the keystane of the brig."

On the common, about half-way between Port Elizabeth and Walmer, there is a little group of Hottentot huts, shaped like large bee-hives, and made of the strangest building-material I ever saw, *i.e.*, a thick mass of the oldest and filthiest rags imaginable. How they hold together has always been a mystery to me; for they flap and flutter ominously in the almost incessant wind, and seem threatening to wing their way across the common and invade the verandahs and gardens of Walmer. Although I have ventured into a good many queer human habitations in different parts of the world, I have never felt inclined to explore the interior of one of these huts, which look as forbidding as their ugly, yellow-skinned inmates. There is no window, no proper outlet for smoke, no room for any one of average figure to stand upright, and the hole which serves as a door is much too low for any more dignified entrance than on all fours— an attitude which, though quite worth while when threading the passages of the Great Pyramid, would hardly be repaid by the sight of the Hottentot in his home; and by the possible acquaintance of creeping, crawling and hopping legions. Numbers of dirty, monkey-like children, and ugly, aggressive dogs of the pariah type, swarm round these huts; the dogs often taking the trouble to pursue the passer-by a long distance on his way, irritating his horse and himself by their clamour, and always keeping just out of reach of the whip.

With the exception of the few remaining Bushmen, the Hottentots are the ugliest and most degraded of all the South African natives. The Kaffirs are much pleasanter to look at, some of the young girls being rather nice-looking, with graceful figures, on which blankets of a beautiful artistic terra-cotta colour are draped in folds worthy of an Arab *burnous*. Occasionally some of the red ochre with which the blankets are coloured is daubed over the face and head, the effect being rather startling. The slender, bronze-like arms are often completely hidden from wrist to elbow by a long spirally-twisted brass wire, looking like a succession of the thinnest bangles quite close together.

We found a comfortable little furnished house at Walmer, in which we spent the first five months after our arrival. It was just a convenient size for our small party, consisting, besides my husband and myself, of our two English servants, and Toto, a beautiful collie. The rooms were all on the ground floor; shaded, and indeed almost darkened, by a broad verandah running the whole length of the front. This absence of sufficient light in nearly all colonial houses strikes the new-comer unpleasantly; but one gets used to it, and in the heat and strong glare of the Cape summer the darkened rooms are restful and comforting. At one end of our verandah we made a little fernery, which we kept green and bright with trophies brought home from some of our longer walks and rides—also an aviary, the little inhabitants of which kept up a constant chorus, always pleasant to hear, and never loud enough to be troublesome. The Cape canary is a greenish bird, with a very pretty soft note, quite different from the piercing screech of his terrible yellow brother in English homes. Another soft-voiced little singer is the *rooibeck*, or red-beak, a wee thing very like an avadavat; a few goldfinches completed our collection, and all were very tame and happy in their little home. The broad leaves of two fine banana-plants shaded birds and ferns from the sun, which otherwise would have beaten in on them too fiercely through the window of the verandah. A banana-plant is a delightful thing to cultivate; it grows so rapidly, and is so full of health and strength; and the unfolding of each magnificent leaf is a new pleasure.

We were within a short walk of our friends' house; and during the frequent absences of T——, my husband, often away for several weeks at a time while searching in different parts of the country for a suitable farm, it was very pleasant for me to have kind neighbours so near, and a bright welcome always awaiting me. Their garden was a large and beautiful one, and its luxuriance of lovely flowers, roses especially, gave ample evidence of their mistress's own care and love for them. Nearly all the houses in Walmer have good gardens, enclosed by the prettiest of hedges, sometimes of pomegranate, plumbago, or passion flowers, but most often of tall American aloes, round the sweet flowers of which the pretty honey-suckers—magnified humming-birds, substantial instead of insect-like—are continually hovering, their jewelled dresses of green, red, and yellow flashing in the sun at every turn of their rapid flight. Close under the hedge, and shaded by the aloe's blue-green spikes, the white arums grow in the thickest profusion. No dining-table in Walmer need be without a simple and beautiful decoration, for if there is no time for a ramble in search of flowers on the surrounding common, you need only run out and pick a few arums from the nearest hedge or small stream; and a few of them go a long way.

But the treasures of the common are endless; and first and loveliest among them all is the little "wax-creeper,"* than which, tiny as it is, I do not think a more perfect flower could be imagined. It is as modest as a little violet; and you have to seek it out in its hiding-places under the thick foliage of the bushes, round the stems of which it twines so tightly that it is a work of some time to disentangle it. You also get many scratches during the process, for it loves to choose as its protectors the most prickly plants; but when at last you hold the delicate wreath in your hands, and look into its minute beauties—the graceful curves of the slender stalk and tendrils, no two of which ever grow alike; the long, narrow, dark-green leaves; and the clusters of brilliant, carmine-tinted flowers, each like a tiny, exquisitely-shaped vase cut out in glistening wax—you are amply rewarded. It is indeed one of the masterpieces of nature, and the first sight of it was a pleasure I can never forget.

This little flower does not bear transplanting. We often tried to domesticate it in our garden, but the plants invariably died. It was quite the rarest of all our flowers. We have never seen it anywhere but about Walmer, and there it grows only in small patches; five

* *Microloma lineare.*

or six plants close together, and then perhaps no more of them to be seen during the whole of a long walk.

Another of our favourites was the *aantblom,* a kind of ixia, whose lovely flowers range through all possible shades of rose-colour and orange, from the deepest to the palest tints of pink and yellow, down to the purest white. A large bouquet of nothing but these delicate, fragile-looking blossoms, each one of a different shade, brought to us by some little neighbours soon after our arrival, was a delightful surprise. So also was the first finding of the sweet Cape jessamine growing wild; but this is one of the rarer plants.

Then there is the scarlet heath; its cluster of large, velvet-like flowers so vivid in colouring as to look like a flame of fire when the sun comes glancing through it. It is the most beautiful of all the Cape heaths, numerous and lovely as they are—though a delicately-shaded pink and white one comes very near it in beauty. The blue lobelias grow profusely all over the common; they are much larger and finer than those in English gardens, and are of the deepest ultra-marine, only a few here and there being a very pretty pale blue. Occasionally—but this is very rare—you find a pure white lobelia. Another flower of our home gardens, the gazania, is very plentiful, the ground being everywhere studded with its large, bright orange-coloured stars.

Pink and white *immortelles,* gladioli, ixias, and irises of all kinds abound; some of the latter are tiny specimens, yet they are pencilled with all the same delicate lines as the larger sorts, though on so small a scale that you almost need a magnifying glass to enable you to see all their beauties. Then there are the Natal lilies, growing in large round clusters, each in itself sufficient to fill a flower-vase; you have but to break a thick, succulent stem, and a perfect, ready-made bouquet of pink, sweet-scented flowers is in your hand.

Some of the plants about Walmer are more curious than beautiful; one especially—which, not knowing its real name,* we called "the upholstery flower"—is like an enormous tassel of red or pink fringe, gaudily ornamented outside with a stiff pattern in green and brown. It is about seven or eight inches long, solid and heavy in proportion; and looks as if in the fitness of things it ought to be at the end of a thick red and green cord looping up the gorgeous curtains of an American hotel. The flower is shaped like a gigantic thistle, but the plant on which it grows is a shrub, with a hard, woody stem, and laurel-like leaves. These are only a few specimens of the common's wealth of flowers; each time we went out we brought home a different collection, and our little rooms were bright with that intensity of colouring which makes the great difference between these children of the sun and the flora of colder climates.

A search for flowers on the common, or, indeed, a walk anywhere about Walmer, is attended by one very unpleasant penalty—you invariably come home covered with ticks. There are several varieties of these tor-

* We have since found that this plant is a *Protea*.

mentors; the tiny, almost invisible ones being by far the worst and most numerous, and their bites, or rather their presence beneath one's skin, causing intense irritation. The large ticks, though they do not confine their attentions wholly to animals, are much more troublesome to them than to the human race, and our poor horses, dog, and other creatures suffered terribly from their attacks. One day, soon after our arrival, I was much amused by the clumsy antics of a number of fowls, which were continually jumping up and pecking at some cattle grazing near. On investigation, I found that they were regaling on the fat ticks with which the poor animals were covered; and our appetite for the Walmer poultry was considerably lessened by the discovery. Ticks abound everywhere along the coast, but as soon as you move inland you are free from the torment.

We had not been very long in Walmer before T—— commenced his ostrich-farming with the purchase of forty-nine young birds, most of them only a few months old, and all wearing the rough, black and grey plumage which, under the name of "chicken-feathers," forms the ostrich's clothing during the first three or four years of his life. We kept them at night in a small enclosure near the house, and during the daytime they grazed on the common, herded by a troublesome little Kaffir boy, who required more looking after than all his charges. The business of counting the latter when they were brought home in the evening was by no means so easy as one would imagine, for the tiresome birds did all in their power to hinder it, and if quiet enough before, seemed always prompted by some mischievous demon to begin moving about as soon as the counting commenced; then, just when we were about half "through"—to use a convenient Americanism—they would get so hopelessly mixed up that we had to begin all over again.

One day T—— and I had the excitement of an ostrich-hunt on horseback. One of our birds, which was much larger than any of the others, being nearly full-grown, and which had to be kept separate lest he should ill-treat his weaker brethren, had got away, and we had a long ride after him; T—— following him up by his *spoor*, or footprints, with as unerring an eye as that of a Red Indian, until at last we were rewarded by the sight of a small head and long snake-like neck above the distant bushes. Then came the very enjoyable but somewhat difficult work of driving our prisoner home. He would trot before us quietly enough for a while, with his curious springy step, till he thought we were off our guard, when he would make an abrupt and unexpected run in the wrong direction; and a prompt rush, like that of the *picador* in a bull-fight, was necessary to cut off his retreat. The horses quite understood what they had to do, and seemed to enter into the spirit of it, and enjoy it as we did.

CHAPTER II.

SOME OF OUR PETS.

Friendliness of South African birds and beasts—Our Secretary bird—Ungainly appearance of Jacob—His queer ways—Tragic fate of a kitten—A persecuted fowl—Our Dikkops—A baby buffalo—Wounded buffalo more dangerous than lion—A lucky stumble—Hunter attacked by "rogue" buffalo—A midnight ride—Followed by a lion—Toto—A pugnacious goose—South African climate dangerous to imported dogs—Toto and the crows—Animals offered by Moors in exchange for Toto.

SOUTH AFRICA is the land of pet animals. The feathered and four-footed creatures are all delightful. They have the quaintest and most amusing ways, and they are very easily tamed. The little time and attention which in a busy colonial home can be spared for the pets is always repaid a hundredfold; and often you are surprised to find how quickly the bird or beast which only a few days ago was one of the wild creatures of the *veldt*—torn suddenly from nest or burrow, and abruptly turned out from the depths of a sack or of a Hottentot's pocket into a human home—has become an intimate friend, with a clearly-marked individual character, most interesting to study, and quite different from those of all its fellows, even of the same kind. On one point, however, the whole collection is sure to be unanimous, and that is a strong feeling of rivalry, and jealousy of one another, each one striving to be first in the affections of master and mistress. A great fondness for and sympathy with animals is not the least among the many tastes which T—— and I have in common; and in our up-country home, far off as we were from human neighbours, we were always surrounded by numbers of animal and bird friends.

We began to form the nucleus of our small menagerie while still at Walmer; and one of our first acquisitions was a secretary bird. The friends near whom we lived possessed three of these creatures, which had all been found, infants together, in one nest on an ostrich farm near Port Elizabeth; and to my great delight, one of them was given to us. "Jacob," as we named him, turned out a most amusing pet. His personal appearance was decidedly comical; reminding us of a little old-fashioned man in a grey coat and tight black knee-breeches; with pale flesh-coloured stockings clothing the thinnest and most angular of legs, the joints of which might have been stiff with chronic rheumatism, so slowly and cautiously did Jacob bend them when picking anything up, or when settling himself down into his favourite squatting attitude. Not by any means a nice old man did Jacob resemble, but an old reprobate, with evil-looking eye, yellow parchment complexion, bald head, hooked nose and fiendish grin; with his shoulders shrugged up, his hands tucked away under his coat-tails, and several

JACOB.

TOTO.

pens stuck behind his ear. Altogether an uncanny-looking creature, and one which, had he appeared in England some two or three centuries ago, would have stood a very fair chance of being burned alive in company with the old witches and their cats; indeed, he looked the part of a familiar spirit far better than the blackest cat could possibly do.

Yet with all his diabolical appearance, Jacob was very friendly and affectionate, and soon grew most absurdly tame—too tame, in fact. He would come running to us the moment we appeared in the verandah, and would follow us about the garden, nibbling like a puppy at our hands and clothes. He would walk, quite uninvited, into the house, where his long-legged ungainly figure looked strangely out of place, and where he was much too noisy to be allowed to remain, although the broadest of hints in the shape of wet bath-sponges, soft clothes-brushes, Moorish slippers, and what other harmless missiles came to hand, were quite unavailing to convince him he was not wanted. The noisy scuffle and indignant gruntings attendant on his forcible expulsion had hardly subsided before he would reappear, walking sedately in at the first door or window available, as if nothing had happened.

His objectionable noises were very numerous; and some of them were unpleasantly suggestive of a hospital. He would commence, for instance, with what seemed a frightful attack of asthma, and would appear to be very near the final gasp; then for about ten minutes he would have violent and alarming hiccups;

the performance concluding with a repulsively realistic imitation of a consumptive cough, at the last stage. His favourite noise of all was a harsh, rasping croak, which he would keep up for any length of time, and with the regularity of a piece of clockwork; this noise was supposed to be a gentle intimation that Jacob was hungry, though the old impostor had probably had a substantial feed just before coming to pose as a starving beggar under our windows. The monotonous grating sound was exasperating; and, when driven quite beyond endurance, T—— would have recourse to extreme measures, and would fling towards Jacob a large dried puff-adder's skin, one of a collection of trophies hanging on the walls of our cottage. The sight of this always threw Jacob into a state of abject terror. He seemed quite to lose his wits, and would dance about wildly, jumping up several feet from the ground in a grotesque manner; till at last, grunting his loudest, and with the pen-like feathers on his head bristling with excitement, he would clear the little white fence, and go off at railway speed across the common, where he would remain out of sight all the rest of the day; only returning at dusk to squat solemnly for the night in his accustomed corner of the garden.

His dread of the puff-adder's skin inclined us to doubt the truth of the popular belief in the secretary's usefulness as a destroyer of snakes, on account of which a heavy fine is imposed by the Cape Government on any one found killing one of these birds. I certainly do not think Jacob would have faced a full-grown puff-adder, though we once saw him kill and eat a small young one in the garden, beating it to death with his strong feet, and then swallowing it at one gulp. He was like a boa-constrictor in his capacity for "putting himself outside" the animals on which he fed—lizards, rats, toads, frogs, fat juicy locusts, young chickens, alas! and some of the smaller pets if left incautiously within his reach, even little kittens —all went down whole. The last-named animals were his favourite delicacy, and he was fortunate enough while at Walmer to get plenty of them. His enormous appetite, and our difficulty in satisfying it, were well known in the neighbourhood, and the owners of several prolific cats, instead of drowning the superfluous progeny, bestowed them on us as offerings to Jacob. They were killed and given to him at the rate of one a day. Once, however, by an unlucky accident, one of them got into his clutches without the preliminary knock on the head; and the old barbarian swallowed it alive. For some minutes we could hear the poor thing mewing piteously in Jacob's interior, while he himself stood there listening and looking all round in a puzzled manner, to see where the noise came from. He evidently thought there was another kitten somewhere, and seemed much disappointed at not finding it.

One day, when there had been a great catch of rats, he swallowed three large ones in succession, but these were almost too much even for him; the tail of the last rat protruded from his bill, and it was a long time before it quite disappeared from view. The butcher had orders to bring liberal supplies for Jacob every day, and the greedy bird soon learned to know the hour at which he called. He would stand solemnly looking in the direction from which the cart came, and as soon as it appeared, he would run in his ungainly fashion to meet it.

Jacob was largely endowed with that quality which is best expressed by the American word "cussedness;" and though friendly enough with us, he was very spiteful and malicious towards all other creatures on the place. He grew much worse after we went to live up-country, and became at last a kind of feathered Ishmael; hated by all his fellows, and returning their dislike with interest. Some time after we settled on our farm we found that he had been systematically inflicting a cruel course of ill-treatment on one unfortunate fowl, which, having been chosen as the next victim for the table, was enclosed, with a view to fattening, in a little old packing-case with wooden bars nailed across the front. Somehow, in spite of abundant mealies and much soaked bread, that fowl never would get fat, nor had his predecessor ever done so; we had grown weary of feeding up the latter for weeks with no result, and in despair had killed and eaten him at last—a poor bag of bones, not worth a tithe of the food he had consumed. And now here was another, apparently suffering from the same kind of atrophy; the whole thing was a puzzle to us, until one day the mystery was solved, and Jacob stood revealed as the author of the mischief. He had devised an ingenious way of persecuting the poor prisoner, and on seeing it we no longer wondered at the latter's careworn looks. Jacob would come up to his box, and make defiant and insulting noises at him—none could do this better than he—until the imbecile curiosity of fowls prompted the victim to protrude his head and neck through the bars; then, before he had time to draw back, Jacob's foot would come down with a vicious dab on his head. The foolish creature never seemed to learn wisdom by experience, though he must have been nearly stunned many times, and his head all but knocked off by Jacob's great powerful foot and leg; yet as often as the foe challenged him, his poor simple face would look inquiringly out, only to meet another buffet. As he would not take care of himself, we had to move him into a safe place; where he no longer died daily, and was able at last to fulfil his destiny by becoming respectably fat.

One day T—— returned from bathing, his Turkish towel, instead of being as usual filled with blue lotus for the dining-table, showing very evident signs of living contents; and two of the queerest little birds came tumbling out of it. They were young dikkops, a little covey of which he had surprised near his bathing-place. They possessed very foolish, vacant faces; and their large, round, bright yellow eyes were utterly void of expression, just as if a bird-stuffer had furnished them with two pairs of glass eyes many sizes too large. Their great thick legs, on the enormously swollen-looking knee-joints of which they squatted in a comical manner, were just as much out of proportion as the eyes, and of the same vivid yellow; indeed, the bird-stuffer seemed to have finished off his work with a thick coating of the brightest gamboge over legs and bill. They had no tail to speak of, and their soft plumage was of all different shades of brown and grey, very prettily marked. The dikkop (a Dutch name, meaning "thickhead"), is a small kind of bustard, and is by far the best of the many delicious game-birds of South Africa. It is a nocturnal bird, sleepy during the daytime, but lively and noisy at night—as we soon found to our discomfort. Not being able to decide at once on a place for our newly-acquired specimens, we put them into our bedroom for the first night, but they were soon awake—so, alas! were we—and their plaintive cry, sounding incessantly from all parts of the room as they ran restlessly to and fro, speedily obliged us to turn them out. We found permanent quarters for them at the end of the verandah, opposite the fernery, where my American trunks—too large to go into the house—had been placed. These we arranged to form a little enclosure, in which the dikkops were safe from the voracious Jacob, who would soon have swallowed them, legs and all, if he had had the chance. One, evidently the smallest and weakest of the covey, we named Benjamin; but, unlike his Scriptural namesake, he received rather a smaller than a larger portion of the good things of this world, the greedy Joseph taking advantage of his own superior size and strength to get the lion's share of all the food, and Benjamin meekly submitting; till we interfered, and by separating the two at feeding-time ensured an equal division. Joseph's general conduct was cruel and unbrotherly; and when one day, during the process of packing to move up-country, he came to an untimely end, being accidentally crushed under the heaviest "Saratoga," we naturally expected Benjamin to rejoice. Instead of this, however, the little fellow pined and fretted; refusing to eat, and calling incessantly with his little mournful cry of three soft musical notes in a minor key, as if hoping to bring back his oppressor—from whom he ought to have been thankful to be free—and at the end of two days he also was dead.

During one of T——'s journeys up-country he made a strange purchase, which he forwarded at once to me by train. It was a baby buffalo, which had been taken alive by the hunters who shot its mother. The buffalo being a rare animal in the Cape Colony, we looked on this little specimen as a great acquisition; and, had he lived, he would have been a very valuable, though perhaps in time somewhat formidable addition to the menagerie; but the railway officials to whose care he was consigned being no exception to the generality of Cape colonists—whose usual way of doing business is to let things take care of themselves—the poor little fellow was put into the train without being fastened or secured in any way, and the jolting he received *en route* knocked him about so that he arrived in a very sad state, with his head cut and bleeding in several places; and did not live many days.

The buffalo is considered by all hunters a far more dangerous animal to encounter than the lion, and almost as formidable as the elephant or rhinoceros. When wounded, he has an ugly trick of lying in wait, hidden in the bush, with only his nose out; and turning the tables on the pursuer by making an unexpected charge. Many hunters have been killed in this manner by infuriated buffaloes.

When T—— was hunting in the interior some years before, a friend who was there with him met with an exciting adventure. Having come across a herd of buffaloes he fired into the midst of them; then, unaware that he had wounded one of the animals, he rode in pursuit of the herd. On coming up with them, he dismounted, and was just preparing to fire again, when a shout from his brother, who was behind, made him look round, just in time to see the wounded buffalo, which had emerged from the bush, charging him furiously. He gave him both barrels, each shot striking him in the centre of the forehead; but, as the buffalo always charges with his nose in the air, both bullets glanced off, and Mr. B—— escaped only by a quick jump on one side. The buffalo passed him; then turning round, tossed and killed the horse. The next shot finished the buffalo's career; and on the great head, which has been kept as a trophy, are the marks of the two first bullets, showing how calm was the presence of mind, and how true the aim, in that moment of danger.

Another of T——'s hunting companions, chased in a

similar manner by a wounded buffalo, owed his life to a lucky stumble, which so astonished the animal that he stood still for a few seconds staring at the prostrate figure; giving the hunter time to get up and take refuge behind a tree, from whence he shot his assailant.

The most dangerous buffaloes are the old solitary bulls which have been turned out of the herd; they become as artful and malicious as rogue elephants, and often hide in the bush when they get your wind, to rush out on you unexpectedly. On another of T——'s hunting expeditions, on the river Sabie, not far from Delagoa Bay, one of the party was walking quietly along with his rifle over his shoulder, when he was suddenly attacked by one of these "rogues," and so frightfully gored that for a time he was not expected to live. T—— started off at once to fetch a doctor; and rode all through the night, steering his course by the stars, to an encampment which most fortunately happened to be within about thirty miles. It was that of a party who were bringing up a number of *mitrailleuses* and other arms, taken in the Franco-Prussian war and presented by Germany to the Transvaal Government. In the camp there were an immense number of donkeys, which were used for the transport of the guns; and when one commenced braying, all the others immediately following suit, it was a Pandemonium which made night hideous indeed. On retracing his course the next day, accompanied by the doctor, T—— saw by the spoor that during that midnight ride he had been followed by a lion.

And now, though the transition seems rather an abrupt one from savage beasts to the sweetest and gentlest of domestic pets, our dear old dog Toto deserves a little notice. We brought him from England with us—he is a dog of Kent, being a native of the Weald—and when put on board the steamer at Southampton he was not many months old. He still had the blunt nose and thick paws of puppyhood; also its mischievous little needle-like teeth, with which he ate off the straps of our portmanteaus, and, when allowed an occasional run on deck, did considerable damage to the Madeira chairs of the passengers. Fortunately he was so general a favourite that his iniquities were overlooked. The children on board were especially fond of him, and would often petition for him to be let loose, to join in their games. He seemed to grow up during the voyage—possibly the sea air hastened his development—and he had almost attained full size and perfect proportions by the time we landed in Cape Town; he, poor fellow, being in such wild delight at finding himself again on *terra firma* and released from the narrowness of ship life, that he was quite mad with excitement, jumping and dragging at his chain, and knocking us nearly off our legs, besides involving us and himself in numerous entanglements with the legs of others. We had to be perpetually apologizing for his conduct, and really felt quite ashamed of him.

He is a large black-and-tan collie; with a soft glossy coat, a big black feather of a tail, and the most superb white frill; of which latter he is justly proud, drawing himself up to show it off to the best advantage whenever it is stroked or admired. Altogether he is a very vain dog, quite conscious of his good looks. His big, honest, loving brown eyes have none of that sly, shifty look which gives a treacherous appearance to so many collies; his face, which is as good and kind as it is pretty, has a great range of expression, and it is wonderful to see how instantly it will change from a benevolent smile, or even a downright laugh, to a pathetic, deeply injured, or scornful look, if Toto considers himself slighted or insulted. We have to study his feelings carefully, for he is proud and sensitive even beyond the usual nature of collies; and if we have been unfortunate enough to offend him—as often as not quite unintentionally—he will give us the cut direct for several days; repelling all advances with the most freezing indifference, and plainly, though always politely, for he is a thorough gentleman, intimating his wish to drop our acquaintance.

Sometimes we are puzzled to know why Toto is haughty and distant towards us, or ignores our existence; and, on looking back, recall perhaps that so long ago as the day before yesterday one of us, in the hurry of daily work, finding his large form obstructing the door through which we had to pass, told him, somewhat impatiently, to get out of the way.

Or perhaps—worse still—we may have laughed at him. Possibly the mouse he was chasing on the veldt popped into the safety of a hole just as he had all but caught it, and we unfeelingly made a joke of his disappointment—or, in his excessive zeal to hold himself very upright when sitting up to beg at dinner, dear Toto may have leaned back just a little too far and rolled over on to his back; a painful position for so majestic an animal, and one which ought to have commanded respectful silence, instead of provoking an unkind laugh. This misfortune has happened several times to poor Toto, especially during the process of learning his threefold trick of sitting up to beg, "asking"—with a little short bark—for bone or biscuit, and finally catching the contribution in his mouth. It is really difficult to refrain from laughing at his sudden collapse, preceded as it always is by an extra self-satisfied look—just the expression of the dog in Caldecott's "House that Jack built," as he sits smiling and all-unconscious of the cow coming up behind to toss him. A conceited protrusion of Toto's big white shirt-frill is usually the occasion of falling, and no doubt he deserves to be laughed at; but the poor fellow's evident distress, and his "countenance more in sorrow than in anger" at our cruel mirth, have led us to make great efforts to keep our gravity, and, with true politeness, to pretend not to see him.

Though Toto is not generally a demonstrative dog, there is no mistake about his affection for us; he shows it in many quiet little sympathetic ways, and seems even more human than the generality of collies. He has constituted himself my special guardian and protector, and though at all times a very devoted attendant, he would always take extra care of me whenever, during T——'s journeys about the country, I was left at home alone. Then the faithful old fellow would not leave me for an instant. The silent sympathy with which he thrust his nose lovingly into my hand cheered the dreary moment when, after watching T—— out of sight, I turned to walk back to the lonely house; and his quiet unobtrusive presence enlivened all the weeks of solitude. He would lie at my feet as I sat working or writing; follow me from room to room or out of doors, always close at my heels; and curl himself up to sleep under my bed, when at any time during the night the slightest word or movement on my part would produce a responsive "tap, tap," of his tail upon the floor. And when his master returned, he always seemed to look to him for approbation; his whole manner expressing his pride in the good care he had taken of house and mistress.

Our garden at Walmer was constantly invaded by neighbouring fowls and ducks, which would lie in wait outside, ready to slip in the instant the little gate was left open; the fowls of course found plenty of occupation among the flowers; while the ducks would at once make for a large tub, generally full of photographic prints taking their final bath under a tap of slowly-trickling water. The horrid birds seemed to take a delight in driving their clumsy bills through the soft, sodden paper; and after several prints from our best negatives had been destroyed, we summoned Toto to our aid. He threw himself with great energy into the work of ridding us of the intruders. He would lie in ambush for them, and when, much to his delight, they appeared inside the gate, he would rush to the attack, chasing first one and then another about the garden till he caught it; then, lifting it and carrying it out in his mouth as gently as a cat carries her kitten, he would deposit it outside, with much angry quacking or frightened screeching from the victim, as the case might be, but without the loss of a feather.

Once he, in his turn, was attacked by a pugnacious goose, which he was endeavouring to drive out of the garden; and which turned on him savagely, keeping up a desperate battle with him for a long time, until it was quite exhausted, and sat down panting. It chased him many times round our small lawn, and once, in its excitement, put its head right into his mouth. Luckily for the goose, Toto was so utterly bewildered by its strange conduct, that he missed the golden opportunity of snapping off the imbecile head so invitingly presented.

He was equally zealous in keeping the garden free from cats; and in pursuit of one of these he actually climbed so far into the lower branches of a tree that his victim, evidently expecting to see him come all the way to the top, gave himself up for lost, and dropped to the ground in a fit.

Imported dogs often die in South Africa; especially if they remain near Port Elizabeth, or if they have distemper, which is much more severe in the colony than it is in Europe. Poor Toto laboured under both these disadvantages; for during our stay at Walmer he was attacked with distemper, and, the summer being also an unusually hot one, everything seemed against him. He was so ill that we quite gave up all hope of saving him, and bitterly regretted having brought him out with us. Just when he was at his worst, however, business called us away for a few days to Cradock, which is some distance inland; and T——, knowing it to be a healthy place for dogs, suggested that we should take the poor creature with us—dying as he seemed to be—on the slight chance that the change of climate might save him. We left him there—parting from him sadly and without much hope of seeing him again; but we were leaving him in the kindest of hands, and, thanks to the careful nursing he received, as well as to the timely change of air, he lived—indeed, I am glad to say, lives still. He remained some months at Cradock, whence from time to time came the good news of his steady improvement, and finally, some time after we had settled up-country, the announcement that he would be sent off to us at the first opportunity.

Then, one day as we sat at dinner, we heard a sudden and startling tumult in the kitchen; the welcoming voices of the servants; a frantic scuffle outside the sitting-room door; and in rushed Toto, handsomer and fuller of life and spirits than ever; whining and howling with delight, and nearly upsetting us, chairs and all, besides endangering everything on the table, as he jumped wildly to lick our faces. He had been brought from Klipplaat by a passing waggon, in the usual "promiscuous" manner in which property, animate as well as inanimate, is delivered at its destination on Cape farms.

After thus paying his footing in South Africa nearly with his life, Toto was thoroughly acclimatized, and passed through several very hot summers on the farm without a day's illness; only showing by increased liveliness his preference for the cooler weather; being very happy on the occasional really cold days of our short winter, and—like everyone else—cross during a hot wind. He has now accompanied us back to England, where—probably on the strength of being an old traveller who has twice crossed the line—he gives himself great airs, and makes no secret of his contempt for the stay-at-home dogs who have not had his advantages. This involves him in many fights; and the brother and sister with whom—having no settled home in England—we have occasionally left him, have several times been threatened with summonses for his misdeeds.

Toto is now getting on in years—those few years, alas! which make up the little span of a dog's life—but he is still lively enough; and the crows at Mogador, where we spent the winter of 1888-89, will long remember the games they have had with that comical foreign dog, so unlike any of the jackal-like creatures to which they were accustomed. They knew him well, and always seemed to look out for him; and, as soon as he emerged from the ugly white-washed gateway of the town, and approached their favourite haunt, the dirty rubbish-heaps just outside the walls, they would fly close up to him, challenging him to catch them.

Undaunted by invariable failure, he was always ready, and would dash noisily after them; while they, enjoying the joke—for every crow is a fellow of infinite jest—flew tantalizingly along close in front of his nose, and only just out of his reach. Sometimes they would settle on the ground a long way off, and—apparently oblivious of him—become so deeply absorbed in searching for the choicest morsels of rubbish that Toto, deluded by the well-acted little play, would make a wild charge. But the artless-looking crows, who all the while were thinking of him, had accurately calculated time and distance; and as he galloped up—confident that this time at least he was really going to catch one—they would allow him to come within an inch of touching them before they would appear to see him at all; then, rising slowly into the air—as if it were hardly worth the trouble to get out of his way—they would hover, croaking contemptuously, above his head, just out of reach of his spring.

And when at last he was tired out with racing after them, and—being, like Hamlet, "fat and scant of breath"—could only fling himself panting on the sand, they would walk derisively all round him; come up defiantly, close to his gasping mouth, and all but perch on him. Before we left, several of the native dogs had learned the game; possibly their descendants will keep it up, and—who knows?—some naturalist of the future may record his discovery of a strange friendship between dogs and crows in Mogador.

From the latter place T—— made several expeditions

to the interior, travelling on foot and in native dress, for the purpose of distributing Arabic Testaments—on one occasion going as far as the city of Morocco. On these trips Toto accompanied his master, and—far from being the object of contempt and aversion, as a dog usually is in Mohammedan lands—was universally admired and coveted by the natives; by some of whom —had T—— not eaten of their bread and salt, thus placing them on their honour—it is extremely likely that he would have been stolen. It was something quite new to them to see a dog actually fond of his master, and treated by the latter as a friend; full of intelligence, too, and altogether different from their own uninteresting dogs; his clever tricks—which seemed to them almost uncanny—earned him many a good feed; and among the variety of animals offered at different times in exchange for him, were two donkeys, a horse, and a young camel.

Toto can boast, too, of having spent many nights in quarters where probably never dog has slept before— *i.e.* in Mohammedan mosques. These were the usual sleeping-places assigned to the travellers by the simple village folk, whose toleration contrasts strongly with the fanaticism of the towns. There the mosques are held very sacred; and for Europeans to look in at their doors, even from across the street, gives great offence.

* * * * *

And now, as I write, the old dog—faithful and friendly as ever—sits up begging; no longer conceitedly and unsteadily as in his youth, but in the more sober fashion of the poor, fat, apoplectic-looking bears at the Zoo; with legs well spread out to afford the firm foundation needed by the portliness of advancing years. His kind eyes are fixed very lovingly and deferentially on the tiny face of his present queen and mistress, the little fair-haired girl who has come to us since we left the Cape; and who, with a regal air of command, holds out her biscuit to the seated Colossus, who, not so long ago, towered above her small head, and bids him "ask for it." Together these two friends and playfellows make so pretty a picture, that we could wish Briton Rivière or Burton Barber were here to see it and give it to the world.

CHAPTER III.

PLANTS OF THE KARROO.

We move up-country—Situation of farm—Strange vegetation of Karroo district—*Karroo* plant—*Fei-bosch*—*Brack-bosch*—Our flowers—*Speckboom*—Bitter aloes—Thorny plants—*Wacht-een-Beetje*—Ostriches killed by prickly pear—Finger-poll—Wild tobacco fatal to ostriches—Carelessness of colonists—Euphorbias—Candle-bush.

OUR five months at Walmer passed so pleasantly, that in spite of my longing to be settled on a place of our own, and the impatience I felt to enter on all the duties and pleasures of farm life among the ostriches, I was really sorry when the time of departure came, and in the beginning of winter—*i.e.* towards the latter part of May—we left the little house, the first home of our married life, and took our journey up-country. We had no very long distance to travel, for the farm in the Karroo district which T—— had chosen was only a day's journey from "The Bay," as Port Elizabeth, like San Francisco, is familiarly called; and instead of being, like many proprietors of farms, quite out of the world, and obliged to drive for two or even three days to reach the railway, we had our choice of two stations; the nearest, Klipplaat, being only fifteen miles from us, and the railway journey not more than eight hours.

Our farm, extending over twelve thousand acres, was situated in a long valley running between two ranges of mountains, the steepness of which rendered enclosing unnecessary in many parts; thus saving much expense in starting the farm, an entirely new one, and chosen purposely by T—— on this account. For it sometimes happens that land on which ostriches have run for years becomes at last unhealthy for the birds. We were in that part of the Karroo which is called the Zwart Ruggens, or "black rugged country;" so named from the appearance it presents when, during the frequent long droughts, the bush loses all its verdure, and becomes outwardly so black and dry-looking that no one unacquainted with this most curious kind of vegetation would suppose it capable of containing the smallest amount of nutriment for ostriches, sheep, or goats. But if you break one of these apparently dried-up sticks, you find it all green and succulent inside, full of a very nourishing saline juice; and thus, even in long droughts which sometimes last more than a year, this country is able to support stock in a most marvellous manner, of which, judging by outward appearance, it certainly does not seem capable. It seems strange that in this land of dryness the plants are so full of moisture; one wonders whence it can possibly have come.

The little *karroo* plant, from which the district takes its name, is one of the best kinds of bush for ostriches, as well as for sheep and goats; it grows in little compact round tufts not more than seven or eight inches from the ground, and though so valuable to farmers, it is but unpretending in appearance, with tiny, narrow leaves, and a little, round, bright yellow flower, exactly resembling the centre of an English daisy after its oracle has been consulted, and its last petal pulled by some enquiring Marguérite.

The *fei-bosch* is another of our commonest and most useful plants; its pinkish-lilac flower is very like that of the portulacca, and its little flat succulent leaves look like miniature prickly pear leaves without the prickles; hence its name, from *Turk-fei*, Turkish fig. When flowering in large masses, and seen at a little distance, the fei-bosch might almost be taken for heather.

The *brack-bosch*, which completes our trio of very best kinds of ostrich-bush, is a taller and more graceful plant than either of the preceding, with blue-green leaves, and blossom consisting of a spike of little greenish tufts; but there are an endless variety of other plants, among which there is hardly one that is not good nourishing food for the birds.

All are alike succulent and full of salt, giving out a crisp, crackling sound as you walk over them; all have the same strange way of growing, each plant a little isolated patch by itself, just as the tufts of wool grow on the Hottentots' heads; and the flowers of nearly all are of the portulacca type, some large, some small, some growing singly, others in clusters; they are of different colours—white, yellow, orange, red, pink, lilac, etc. They are very delicate and fragile flowers;

A. MARTIN, *del.*

Some of the Best Kinds of Ostrich-Bush.
1. BRACK-BOSCH. 2. GHANNA. 3. FEI-BOSCH.

and, pretty as they are, it is useless to attempt carrying them home, for they close up and fade as soon as they are gathered.

Indeed, nearly all the flowers in that part of the world are unsatisfactory; and those few among them which will keep for a very short time in water are almost useless for table decorations, as they seem incapable of adapting themselves to any sort or form of flower-vase. They are pretty enough in themselves; but the large, thick, stubborn stems, all out of proportion with the flowers, refuse to bend themselves to any graceful form or combination; they all seem starting away from one another in an angular, uncomfortable manner, and of course any pretty arrangement of flowers which *will* not arrange *themselves* is impossible. Our thoughts often went back longingly to the flowers of Walmer, compared with which prolific region the Karroo is poverty indeed.

A cineraria, very nearly as large as the cultivated varieties, and of a beautiful deep blue, on which the Dutch have bestowed the euphonious name of *blaauw-blometje* (little blue flower), several tiny irises, and a rather rare bulb, the hyacinth-like blossoms of which, as well as the upper part of the stalk, are of a lovely tint between scarlet and deep rose-colour, and all soft and velvety in texture, are among our prettiest flowers.

Then there are the mimosa's balls of soft, sweet-scented yellow fringe, perfuming the air all round for a long distance, and making the trees seem all of gold when covered with their masses of bloom. Here and there is a Kaffir bean, a shrub with rather handsome large red flowers, but it is not common. There are a good many colourless, insignificant-looking flowers, and some which are quite uncanny; one, especially, with pendent, succulent bells of livid green and dull red, looks worthy to be one of the ingredients of a witch's cauldron. These are all flowers of the plains; the mountains are richer, but their treasures are only to be attained by making rather long excursions up their steep sides, over the roughest and stoniest of ground, and through a tangled mass of vegetation, most of which is very thorny. But even the weariest climb is well repaid on reaching the heights where the wild geraniums grow. The immense round bushes, five or six feet in diameter, and brilliant with great bunches of pink or scarlet flowers, are indeed a lovely sight. A creeping ivy-leaved geranium, and a very pretty pelargonium, which is also a creeper, grow in these same far-off regions; the flower of the latter is of a beautiful rich maroon and cream-colour, its curiously jointed stem and tiny leaves are very succulent, salt to the taste, and strongly scented with the sweet geranium perfume. It is strange to notice how plants which in Europe are neither saline nor particularly succulent, when growing in the Karroo assume the prevailing character of its vegetation.

Large white *marguērites*, growing on a shrub with a hard, woody stem, inhabit the same heights as the geraniums and pelargoniums; all these together would have been invaluable for the brightening of our little rooms, if we could possibly have brought them home. But they are all much too delicate to survive the long walk or ride back, and the only mountain flowers we could reasonably hope to bring home in a presentable condition were the large, bright yellow *immortelles*. The scanty little streams trickling down some of the cool shady *kloofs* between the mountains are the home of a few white arums; and their rocky beds are fringed, though not very abundantly, with maidenhair fern.

The *spekboom*, which is a good-sized shrub, sometimes attaining the height of fifteen or twenty feet, grows plentifully a little way up the mountains; and in very protracted droughts, when the karroo and other bush of the plains begin at last to fail, it is our great resource for the ostriches, which then ascend for the purpose of feeding on it; and though they do not care for it as they do for their usual kinds of food, it is good and nourishing for them. Elephants are very fond of the *spekboom*, but though a few of these animals are still found near Port Elizabeth, there are fortunately none in our neighbourhood to make inroads on the supplies reserved for the ostriches against what certainly in South Africa cannot be called "a rainy day." The *spekboom* has a large soft stem, very thick, round, succulent leaves, and its clusters of star-shaped, wax-like flowers are white, sometimes slightly tinged with pink. There are several plants very closely resembling the *spekboom* ; one with pretty, bright yellow flowers; and one, the soft stem of which, if cut into thin slices, looks exactly like very red salt tongue.

Those unpleasant old acquaintances of childish days, the bitter aloes, are at home in the Karroo in great numbers; and most brilliantly do they light up the somewhat gloomy-looking sides of the mountains in early spring with the great spikes of their shaded scarlet and orange-coloured flowers, looking like gigantic "red-hot poker plants." This African aloe has none of the slender grace of its American relative, and it is only when flowering that it has any claim to beauty; at all other times it is simply a most untidy-looking plant, the thick, clumsy stem for about five or six feet below the crown of leaves being covered with the ragged, decaying remains of former vegetation, suggestive of numberless scorpions and centipedes.

Thorny plants abound, especially on the mountains, where indeed almost every bush which is not soft and succulent is armed with strong, sharp, often cruelly hooked spikes. The *wacht-een-beetje* (wait-a-bit) does not grow in our neighbourhood, but we have several plants which seem to me no less deserving of the name; and often, when held a prisoner on some ingenious arrangement of hooks and spikes viciously pointing in every possible direction, each effort to free myself involving me more deeply, and inflicting fresh damage on clothes and flesh, I should, but for T——'s assurance to the contrary, have quite believed I had encountered it. The constant repairing of frightful "trap-doors" and yawning rents of all shapes and sizes in T——'s garments and in my own, took up a large proportion of time; and often did I congratulate myself on the fact that my riding-habit at least—chosen contrary to the advice of friends at home, who all counselled coolness and lightness above everything—was of such stout, strong cloth as to defy most of the thorns. Any less substantial material would have been reduced to ribbons in some of our rides.

On foot, you are perpetually assailed by the great strong hooks of the wild asparagus, a troublesome enemy, whose long straggling branches trailing over the ground are most destructive to the skirts of dresses; while boots have deadly foes, not only in the shape of rough ground and hard, sharp-pointed stones, but also in that of numerous prickly and scratchy kinds of small bush. At the end of one walk in the *veldt*, the surface of a kid boot is all rubbed and torn into little ragged points, and is never again fit to be seen. Fortunately, in the Karroo, no one is over-particular about such small details.

Among our troublesome plants, one of the worst and most plentiful is the prickly pear; and farmers have indeed no reason to bless the old Dutchwoman who, by simply bringing one leaf of it from Cape Town to Graaff-Reinet, was the first introducer of what has become so great a nuisance. It spreads with astonishing rapidity, and is so tenacious of life that a leaf, or even a small portion of a leaf, if thrown on the ground, strikes out roots almost immediately, and becomes the parent of a fast-growing plant; and it is not without great trouble and expense that farms can be kept comparatively free from it. Sometimes a little party of Kaffirs would be encamped on some part of our land especially overgrown with prickly pears; and there for months together they would be at work, cutting in pieces and rooting out the intruders; piling the disjointed stems and leaves in neatly-arranged stacks, where they would soon ferment and decay. Labour being dear in the colony, the wages of "prickly-pear-men" form a large item in the expenditure of a farm; in many places indeed, where the plants are very numerous, it does not pay to clear the land, which consequently becomes useless, many farms being thus ruined.

Sometimes ostriches, with that equal disregard of their own health and of their possessor's pocket for which they are famous, help themselves to prickly pears, acquire a morbid taste for them, and go on indulging in them, reckless of the long, stiff spikes on the leaves, with which their poor heads and necks soon become so covered as to look like pin-cushions stuck full of pins; and of the still more cruel, almost invisible fruit-thorns which at last line the interior of their throats, besides so injuring their eyes that they become perfectly blind, and are unable to feed themselves.

Many a time has a poor unhappy ostrich, the victim of prickly pear, been brought to me in a helpless, half-dead state, to be nursed and fed at the house. Undaunted by previous experience, I perseveringly tended each case, hoping it might prove the exception to the general rule, but never were my care and devotion rewarded by the recovery of my patient. There it would squat for a few days, the picture of misery; its long neck lying along the ground in a limp, despondent manner, suggestive of the attitudes of seasick geese and ducks on the first day of a voyage. Two or three times a day I would feed it, forcing its unwilling bill open with one hand, while with the other I posted large handfuls of porridge, mealies, or chopped prickly pear leaves in the depths of its capacious letter-box of a throat. All to no purpose; it had made up its mind to die, as every ostrich does immediately illness or accident befalls it, and most resolutely did it carry out its intention.

The prickly pear, mischievous though it is, is not altogether without its good qualities. Its juicy fruit, though rather deficient in flavour, is delightfully cool and refreshing in the dry heat of summer; and a kind of treacle, by no means to be despised at those not infrequent times when butter is either ruinous in price or quite unattainable, is made from it. A strong, coarse spirit, equal to the *aguardiente* of Cuba in horrible taste and smell, is distilled from prickly pears; and though to us it seemed only fit to be burned in a spirit-lamp, when nothing better could be procured, it is nectar to the Boers and Hottentots, who drink large quantities of it. Great caution is needed in peeling the prickly pear, the proper way being to impale the fruit on a fork or stick while you cut it open and remove the skin. On no account must the latter be touched with the hands, or direful consequences will ensue. To the inexperienced eye the prickly pear looks innocent enough; with its smooth, shiny skin, suggestive only of a juicy interior, and telling no tale of lurking mischief—yet each of those soft-looking little tufts, with which at regular intervals it is dotted, is a quiver filled with terrible, tiny, hair-like thorns, or rather stings; and woe betide the fingers of the unwary "new chum," who, with no kind friend at hand to warn him, plucks the treacherous fruit. He will carry a lively memento of it for many days.

My first sad experience of prickly pears was gained, not in South, but in North Africa. Landing with a friend in Algiers some time ago, our first walk led us to the fruit market, where, before a tempting pile of *figues de Barbarie*, we stopped to quench the thirst of our thirty-six hours' passage. The fruit was handed to us, politely peeled by the Arab dealer; and thus, as we made our first acquaintance with its delightful coolness, no suspicion of its evil qualities entered our minds. And when, a few days later, adding the excitement of a little trespassing to the more legitimate pleasures of a country ramble, we came upon a well-laden group of prickly pear bushes, we could not resist the temptation to help ourselves to some of the fruit—and woeful was the result. Concentrated essence of stinging-nettle seemed all at once to be assailing hands, lips, and tongue; and our skin, wherever it had come in contact with the ill-natured fruit, was covered with a thick crop of minute, bristly hairs, apparently growing from it, and venomous and irritating to the last degree. Our silk gloves, transformed suddenly into miniature robes of Nessus, had to be thrown away, perfectly unwearable; and the inadvertent use of our pocket-handkerchiefs, before we had fully realized the extent of our misfortune, caused fresh agonies, in which nose as well as lips participated. For many a day did the retribution of that theft haunt us in the form of myriads of tiny stings. It was a long time indeed before we were finally rid of the last of them; and we registered a vow that whatever Algerian fruit we might dishonestly acquire in future, it should not be *figues de Barbarie*.

In dry weather at the Cape these spiteful little stings do not even wait for the newly-arrived victim; but fly about, light as thistle-down, ready to settle on any one who has not learned by experience to give the prickly pear bushes a wide berth.

The leaves of the prickly pear are good for ostriches and cattle, though the work of burning off the thorns and cutting the leaves in pieces is so tedious that it is only resorted to when other food becomes scarce. One kind, the *kahlblad*, or "bald leaf," has no thorns. It is comparatively rare, and farmers plant and cultivate it as carefully as they exterminate its troublesome relative.

Another kind of cactus, which, if the beautiful forms in Nature were utilized for artistic purposes half as much as they deserve to be, would long since have been recognized as a most perfect model for a graceful branched candlestick, is used as food for cattle during long droughts, being burnt and cut up in the same manner as the prickly pear. When the plant is in flower, each branch of the candlestick seems tipped with a bright yellow flame.

Another of our many eccentric-looking plants, the *finger-poll*, is also used in very dry seasons to feed cattle; the men who go about the country cutting it up being followed by the animals, which are very fond of it, but which, owing to its excessive toughness, are unable to bite it off. It grows close to the ground; its perfect circle of thick, short fingers, rather like gigantic asparagus, radiating stiffly from the centre. How the cattle manage to eat it without serious consequences has always been a matter of wonder to me, for the whole plant is filled with a thick, white, milky juice, which when dry becomes like the strongest indiarubber. We often used this juice for mending china, articles of jewellery, and many things which defied coaguline, to which, indeed, we found it superior.

One of our plants always reminded me of those French sweets, threaded on a stiff straw, which often form a part of the contents of a bon-bon box. The thick, succulent leaves, shaded green and red, with a frosted, sparkling surface which increases the resemblance to the candied sweets, and all as exactly alike in shape and size as if made in one mould, are threaded like beads at equal distances along the stem, which passes through a little round hole in the very centre of each. They can all be taken off and threaded on again just as they were before.

Close to the ground, and growing from a little round root apparently belonging to the bulbous tribe, you sometimes—though only rarely—see a tiny mass of soft, curling fibres, delicate and unsubstantial-looking as a little green cloud. Even the foliage of asparagus would look coarse and heavy if placed beside this really ethereal little plant, which yet is durable, for I have now with me a specimen which, though gathered five years ago, is still quite unchanged.

The wild tobacco is a common—indeed too common—plant in the Karroo; it has clusters of long, narrow, trumpet-shaped flowers, of a light yellow, its leaves are small, and it resembles the cultivated tobacco neither in appearance nor in usefulness. Indeed it is one of our worst enemies, being poisonous to ostriches, which of course—true to their character—lose no opportunity of eating it. We made deadly war upon it, and whenever during our rides about the farm we came upon a clump of its blue-green bushes, we would make up a little bonfire at the foot of each, and burn it down to the ground. But it is tenacious of life, and its roots go down deep, so its career of evil was only cut short for a time. Besides which, our efforts to keep it under were of little avail while our neighbours, "letting things slide," in true colonial fashion, allowed the plants to run wild on their own land; from whence the seeds were always liable to be washed down to us during "a big rain," when the deep *sluits* which everywhere intersect the country become, in a few hours, raging torrents, dashing along at express speed.

Strangely enough, when T——, some years ago, was travelling in Australia, to which country he had brought some ostriches from the Cape, he found that wild tobacco grew nowhere throughout the length and breadth of the land, excepting just in the very region in which the birds had been established. During that trip he also found that the "salt-bush" of Australia, which is there considered the best kind of food for sheep, is almost identical with the brack-bosch of the Cape Colony, the only difference being that it grows higher. We have also seen the same bush growing in Algeria, and near Marseilles.

On the lower slopes of some of our mountains grow tall euphorbias, shooting up straight and stiff as if made of metal, and branching out in the exact form of the Jewish candlestick sculptured on the arch of Titus in Rome. Some of these euphorbias attain the height of forty feet—quite important dimensions in that comparatively treeless land. They impart an air of melancholy and desolation to the landscape; and look particularly weird and uncanny when, on a homeward ride, you pass through a grove of them at dusk.

One more queer plant in conclusion of these slight and very unscientific reminiscences of our flora, which I trust may never meet the eye of any botanist. The *kerzbosch*, or candle-bush, a stunted, thorny plant, if lighted at one end when in the green state, will burn steadily just like a wax candle, and is used as a torch for burning off the thorns of prickly pear, etc.

CHAPTER IV.

OUR LITTLE HOME.

Building operations—A plucking—Ugliness of Cape houses—Our rooms—Fountain in sitting-room a failure—Drowned pets—Decoration of rooms—Colonist must be Jack-of-all-trades—Cape waggons—Shooting expeditions—Strange tale told by Boer.

On our first arrival in the Karroo we were unable to take up our abode at once on our own farm; the best of the three small Dutch houses on it being little better than a hut, and consisting but of two small and badly-built rooms; with mud floors and smoke-blackened reed ceilings, as far removed from the horizontal as the roughly-plastered walls, which bulged and retreated in all unexpected directions, were from the perpendicular —the whole architecture, if so pretentious a term may be used, being entirely innocent of any approach to a straight line or correct angle. We at once commenced building operations; in the meanwhile renting a little house which happened to be vacant on the next farm, about an hour's rough, but pretty ride from our own. Now came a busy time for T——, and for his manager —the latter already installed, uncomfortably enough, in the old Dutch house—for besides the brick-making and building, and the deepening of the well near the house, there was, as must always be the case on starting a new farm, much to be done, and everything required to be done at once. T—— spent most of his time at "Swaylands," as we named our farm; and very enjoyable for me were the days when I could spare a few hours from household duties to ride over with him, to watch the progress of the new rooms, or to be initiated into some of the mysteries of ostrich-farming, all delightfully new and strange to me.

The first sight of a plucking interested me especially; and it was not without a proud feeling of ownership that I sat on the ground in one corner of the kraal, or small temporary enclosure, helping to tie up in neat bundles our own first crop of soft, white, black, or grey feathers while watching the busy scene. It all comes back to me now with the clearness of a photograph — the bright, cloudless, metallic-looking South African sky above us; and for a background the long range of rocky mountains, each stain on their rugged sides, each aloe or *spekboom* plant growing on them, sharply defined in that clear atmosphere as if seen through the large end of an opera-glass. In the foreground a forest of long necks, and a crowd of foolish, frightened faces, gaping beaks, and throats all puffed out with air — the latter ludicrous grimace, accompanied sometimes by a short, hollow sound, half grunt, half cough, being the ostrich's mode of expressing deepest disgust and dejection. There is a constant heavy stamping of powerful two-toed feet; an occasional difference of opinion between two quarrelsome birds eager to fight, craning their snake-like necks, hissing savagely, and " lifting up themselves on high," but unable, owing to the closeness with which they are packed, to do each other any injury ; and the real or fancied approach of a dog causes a sudden panic and general stampede of the silly birds into one corner of the kraal, threatening to break down its not very substantial hedge of dry bush—one commotion scarcely having time to subside before another arises.

And through it all, T——, Mr. B——, and our Kaffirs are calmly going in and out among the struggling throng ; all hard at work, the two former steadily and methodically operating with their shears on each bird as in its turn it is tugged along, like a victim to the sacrifice, by three men ; two holding its wings, and the third dragging at its long neck till one fears that with all its kicks, plunges, tumbles, and sudden wild leaps into the air, its flat, brainless little head will be pulled off. One extra-refractory bird, when finally subdued, and helpless in the hands of the pluckers, avenges his wrongs upon the ostrich standing nearest to him in the crowd ; and, for every feather pulled from his own tail, gives a savage nip to the head of his unoffending neighbour, a mild bird, who does not retaliate, but looks puzzled, his own turn not yet having come. It is amusing to watch the rapid retreat of each poor denuded creature when set free from his tormentors. He goes out at the gate looking crestfallen indeed, but apparently much relieved to find himself still alive.

How we enjoyed that day! and how delightful was our ride back to "Hume Cottage" in the evening, with the proceeds of the plucking tied up in two large white bags, and fastened to our saddles; making us look as if we were taking our clothes to the wash. My bundle, by the way, came to grief *en route*, and suddenly — somewhat to the discomposure of my horse — we found ourselves enveloped in a soft snow-storm of feathers, which went flying and whirling merrily away across the *veldt;* many of them, in spite of our prompt dismounting to rush madly hither and thither in pursuit, quite evading all our efforts to catch them.

The modern houses on Cape farms are all built entirely on utilitarian principles, with no thought of grace or beauty; indeed, the square and prosaic proportions of the ordinary packing-case seem to have been chosen as the model in the construction of nearly every room. Even if the inmates had any idea of comfort, or feeling for the picturesque — of both of which they are quite innocent — it would be impossible ever to make such rooms look either home-like or pretty. As it is, they are most often like very uncomfortable schoolrooms.

Our first plan on coming to South Africa was the ambitious one of setting our fellow-colonists a brilliant example by striking out something entirely new in farm architecture; and many times during our stay at Walmer would we talk over the white Algerian house, with the comfort and loveliness of which our ostrich-farm, wherever it might be, was to be transformed into a little oasis in the desert. T—— covered many sheets of writing-paper with designs for the horse-shoe arches; and with neatly-drawn plans for the long, cool Oriental rooms, surrounding the square open court; in the centre of which was to be a fountain with bananas, ferns, blue lotus, and other water-loving plants.

Alas! however; when we did take a farm, we found ourselves obliged after all to sacrifice beauty to usefulness, just like our neighbours. The unlovely Dutch house, incapable as it was of adapting itself to Moorish arches, had to be utilized; the press of other work allowing us no time for pulling down and re-building, neither for indulging in any artistic vagaries; and the two first rooms which—to meet immediate requirements—were added as soon as bricks could be made for them, were, for greater haste, built straight and square, in the true packing-case style. They were the same size as the two old Dutch rooms; flat-roofed like them, and built on to them in a straight line—the four, each with its alternate door and window, reminding us of the rows of little temporary rooms which form the dwellings of railway workmen when a new line is being made, and which are moved on as the work progresses.

After this unpromising beginning, it is needless to say that our idea of building an Algerian house was given up; and though in time we improved the outward appearance of our dwelling; breaking the straightness of its outlines by the addition of a pretty little sitting-room projecting from the front, and of a large bedroom and store at the back; and plastering and whitewashing the dirty old bricks and the too-clean new ones; nothing can ever make it anything but an ugly house as far as the outside is concerned. With the interior, however, we have been more successful; and our sitting-room, now consisting of a T-shaped arrangement of three small rooms thrown into one, is really—considering the roughness of the materials with which we started—a very bright and cosy little nook. It is most quaint and irregular, for one end of it is a room of the crookedly-built Dutch house; and when the strong old wall, three feet thick, dividing the latter from the new part, was knocked away, the old ceiling and floor turned out to be considerably lower than the new. We dignify the deep step thus formed by the name of "the dais."

The latest-added portion of the room—built from T——'s own design—is the prettiest of all; and the bow window at the end, always filled with banana-plants, ferns, creepers, garden and wild flowers, forms quite a little conservatory. Though disappointed of our Moorish court, we could not give up the idea of our fountain without a struggle, and attempted to establish it on a very small scale in this little room; in the cement floor of which, not far from the bow window, we made a round basin some four feet deep, which we filled with water. Then we wrote to Walmer for some roots of our favourite blue lotus; with which, and with the arums' white cups, the surface of the water was to be studded; and by-and-by—we thought—as soon as the

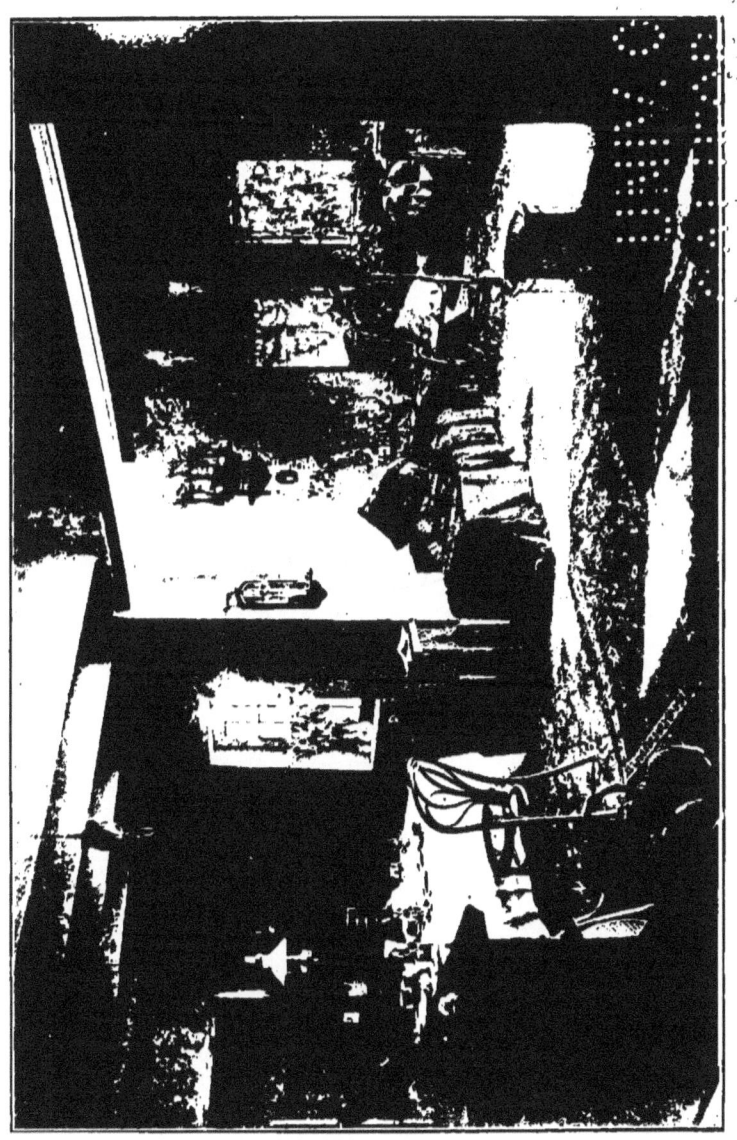

OUR SITTING-ROOM.

completion of more necessary operations should allow leisure for ornamental work, how delightful it would be, on coming in out of the dust and the heat, to hear the sweet, refreshing sound of falling water; and to see the bright drops splashing on the border of maidenhair fern which was to surround the tiny basin.

But, after all, our anticipations were never realized; for we soon saw that it would be necessary to choose between our fountain and our pet animals—so numerous among the latter were cases of "Found Drowned." Our meerkats, in their irrepressible liveliness, were always tumbling in; and, being unable to climb up the straight sides, would swim round and round calling loudly for assistance; but we were not always at hand to play the part of Humane Society, and the losses were many, including—saddest of all—that of a too-inquisitive young ostrich.

Thousands of gnats, too, as noisy and nearly as venomous as mosquitoes, were brought into existence; and, romantic as was the idea of water-plants growing in our little room, it had to be given up; and we contented ourselves with seeing our blue lotus in the form of a dado, on which we stencilled and painted them ourselves in the true Egyptian conventional style, on alternate long and short stalks. We bordered the fireplace, and decorated the tops of the doors, with a few good old tiles from Damascus, Tunis, Algiers, and the Alhambra; three beautiful hand-painted *sarongs*, brought by T—— from Java, formed each as perfect and artistic a *portière* as could be wished, and hid the ugly, ill-made doors; and with Turkish rugs, Oriental embroideries of all kinds, Moorish and Kabyle pottery, Algerian coffee-tables and brackets, ancient Egyptian curiosities, and other trophies of travel, we produced a general effect which—especially in South Africa—was not to be despised.

I have conceitedly said "we," as if I had had a great share in the work, but it was in reality T—— who did it all, and to whose artistic taste the prettiness of our little home is entirely due. The capacity, too, for turning his hand to anything, which makes him so perfect a colonist, was invaluable to us on that out-of-the-way farm; for, there being, after the departure of the itinerant workmen who built our rooms, no painters, glaziers, masons, carpenters, or other such useful people anywhere nearer than Graaff-Reinet—four hours by rail from Klipplaat—all the repairs and improvements of the house devolved on him. One day he would be putting new panes of glass in the windows—the next, bringing a refractory lock into proper working order, or making and putting up bookshelves—then, perhaps, a defective portion of the roof would claim his attention, or he would enter on a long and persevering conflict with a smoky chimney. One of the latter, indeed, carelessly run up by our ignorant builder, was not cured until T—— had taken it all down and built it over again; since which its behaviour has been blameless.

N.B.—When a chimney wants sweeping in the Karroo, the usual mode of procedure is to send a fowl down it.

Our furniture, most of which was of that best kind of all for a hot climate, the Austrian bent wood, arrived in very good condition; and in spite of the rough roads along which the waggon had to bring it from Klipplaat, hardly anything was damaged.

These Cape waggons, clumsy as they look, are splendidly adapted to the abrupt ups and downs of the country over which they travel. They are very long; and are made in such a way that, instead of jolting and jumping up and down as an English waggon, under the trying circumstances of a journey in South Africa, would certainly consider itself justified in doing, they turn and bend about in quite a snake-like manner, and the motion, even on the roughest road, is never unpleasant. They are usually drawn by a span of sixteen or eighteen oxen, sometimes by mules; and very noisily they go along; night—their favourite travelling-time in hot weather—being made truly hideous while a caravan of some four or five of them is coming slowly on, with wheels creaking and groaning in all possible discordant notes, and the Hottentot drivers and *voorloopers*—boys who run in front—cracking their long hide whips, and urging on their animals with more fiendish sounds than ever issued even from Neapolitan throats. One has to get accustomed to the noise; but, apart from this drawback, the waggons are most comfortable for travelling. They are large and spacious, and roofed in by firmly-made tents which afford complete protection from sun and rain; and for night journeys no Pullman car ever offered more luxurious sleeping accommodation than does the *kartel*, a large, strong framework of wood, as wide as a double-bed, suspended inside the tent of the waggon. Across this framework are stretched narrow, interlacing strips of hide; mattresses and rugs are placed on it, and no more comfortable bed could be desired. The goods are all stowed underneath the *kartel*, in the bottom of the waggon.

People often make shooting expeditions to the interior, travelling in waggons and sometimes remaining away a year at a time. T—— has taken several journeys of this kind, and speaks of it as a most enjoyable life. You take a horse or two and a couple of pointers; you get plenty of shooting during the day; and come back to the waggon in the evening to find a bright fire burning near, and dinner being prepared by the servants. The latter camp at night under the waggon. The average distance travelled is twenty-five miles a day. There is no need to take provisions for the cattle, as they are always able to graze on the way; tracts of land, called public outspans, being set apart by Government at convenient distances along the road as halting-places for waggons.

A Boer once told T—— a strange story of how—during one of the numerous wars with the natives—he, his wife, and children were travelling at night, when suddenly, without any apparent cause, the waggon came to a standstill; the oxen, though beaten hard and pulling with all their might, being unable to move it, although the road at that place was perfectly level.

After some delay, the cattle were just as suddenly again able to move the waggon without difficulty ; and the Boer and his family proceeded on their way. They found afterwards that, by this strange interruption to their journey, they had been prevented from encountering an armed party of hostile natives, who just at that time were crossing their road some distance in front of them.

CHAPTER V.

CLIMATE OF THE KARROO.

Cape Colony much abused—Healthy climate—Wonderful cures of consumption—Karroo a good place for sanatorium—Rarity of illness and accidents—The young colonist—An independent infant—Long droughts—Hot winds—Dust storms—Dams—Advantage of possessing good wells—Partiality of thunderstorms—Delights of a brack roof—Washed out of bed—After the rain—Our horses—Effects of rain indoors—*Opslaag*—The Cape winter—What to wear on Karroo farms.

OF all portions of the globe, surely none has ever been so much grumbled at, abused, and despised, both justly and unjustly, as the poor Cape Colony. Hardly any one who has lived under its cloudless skies has a kind word to say for it; indeed, it is quite the usual thing to speak of one's residence in it as of an enforced and miserable exile—a kind of penal servitude—though, strangely enough, most of those who go so rejoicingly home to England, like boys released from school, manage sooner or later to find their way out again; as though impelled by a touch of some such magic as that which is supposed to draw back to the Eternal City those who have once drunk at the Trevi fountain.

One of the legion of grumblers tells you the Cape

Colony is the worst-governed country in the world, which indeed—with the exception, perhaps, of Turkey and Morocco—it undoubtedly is; the grievance of another is that the country in general, and ostrich-farming in particular, is played out, that no more fortunes are to be made, and that life on the farms offers nothing to compensate sufficiently for the numerous discomforts and privations which have to be endured; the heavy import duties and consequent ruinous prices of all the necessaries of life, with the exception of meat, depriving the colonist of even that small consolation of knowing that, though uncomfortable, he is at least economizing. Sybarites accustomed to home comforts make constant comparisons between English and colonial houses, greatly to the disparagement of the latter; epicures complain bitterly of the wearying sameness of the food, resenting most deeply the perpetual recurrence on the table, morning, noon, and night, of the ubiquitous though delicious Angora goat; while ladies are eloquent on the never-ending topics of the bad servants—certainly the worst that can be found anywhere—the difficulties of housekeeping, the rough roads, the inconvenient distance from everywhere, the trouble and delay of getting provisions, etc., sent up to the farms, and, saddest of all, the want of society and the intolerable dulness. In fact, the general opinion seems to be that of Mrs. Jellyby's daughter, that "Africa is a Beast!" You hear so much grumbling, see such bored, dissatisfied faces, and are treated to so many gloomy and desponding views of colonial life, that it is quite a refreshing contrast when you chance to meet an American who is contemptuously jocular on the subject of the ugly scenery, eccentric plants, queer beasts, and general all-pervading look of incompleteness, and who guesses "South Africa was finished off in a hurry late on Saturday night, with a few diamonds thrown in to compensate."

Even the climate comes in for its share of abuse: its long droughts, its hot winds, its incessant sunshine—as if you *could* have too much of that!—and its general dissimilarity to the climate of England—for which surely it ought to be commended,—all are added to the long list of complaints against a land which seems, like the much-abused donkey, to have no friends. And yet that climate, with all its drawbacks and discomforts, is the healthiest in the world; and most especially is the Karroo district the place of all others for invalids suffering from chest complaints. No one need die of consumption, however advanced a stage his disease may have attained, if he can but reach the Cape Colony and *proceed at once inland.* He must not stay near the coast; it would be as well—indeed better—for him to have remained in England to die among friends; for in the moist neighbourhood of the sea the disease cannot be cured, its progress is simply retarded for a while. But a railway journey of only a few hours lands the patient in the very heart of the Karroo; and once in its dry atmosphere, he may hope—nay expect—not a mere prolongation for a few months of such a life as one too often sees sadly ebbing away in Mediterranean winter resorts, but a return to health and strength. Among our Cape acquaintances are some whom T—— knew when, years ago, they landed in the Colony— given up by their doctors at home, and so near the last stage of consumption that on arriving they could not walk on shore, but had to be carried from the vessel— and who are now as strong and well as any of their neighbours. Indeed, on my introduction to more than one of these stout and hearty colonists, I have found it quite impossible to realize that *they*, at any time, could have been consumptive invalids! Unfortunately, too many presume on the completeness of their cure; and, instead of resigning themselves to settling and finding permanent occupation in the colony, as all whose lungs have once been seriously affected ought to do, return to England; and, having grown reckless with long residence in a land where "nothing gives you cold," soon fall victims to their treacherous native climate; the first exposure to its damp chilliness generally bringing back in full force the foe from whose attacks they would always have been safe, had they not left the dry Karroo's protection.

It is a pity European doctors do not know more about this wonderful climate for consumptive patients; and also that so few inducements are held out for the latter to settle in the country. What a splendid plan it would be, and how many valuable lives might be saved, if some clever medical man—himself perhaps just enough of an invalid to prefer living out of England —were to take a large farm in the Karroo, and "run" it as a sanatorium. This could be done without the expenditure of any very large amount of capital, as land can be rented from Government at the rate of a very moderate sum per annum. It would be necessary to choose a farm possessing a good fountain; thus a constant supply of vegetables could be kept up, and herds of cattle, flocks of sheep and Angoras, and plenty of fowls, turkeys, etc., be maintained to provide the establishment with meat, milk, butter, and eggs— rendering it to a great extent self-supporting. The young men could occupy themselves in superintending the farming operations, and thus would not only have plenty to do, but would at the same time be gaining health. A good troop of horses would of course be kept, so that patients might have as much riding and driving as they wished; there would be some shooting, as there are partridges, several birds of the bustard tribe, and a few antelopes; and with a house whose interior presented the comforts of a refined home, with prettily-furnished rooms, and with a good supply of books, papers, and magazines, life in that bright, sunny land might be made pleasant enough. The healthiness of the country is greatly owing, not only to its dryness, but also to the fact of its being a table-land, one thousand feet above the sea; thus the nights are always cool, and one is generally glad of two blankets, even in summer.

Nor is consumption the only enemy who has to retreat powerless before the Karroo's health-giving atmosphere; many other illnesses seem equally unable to obtain a footing in that perfect climate. T——, for instance, who from childhood had been subject to severe attacks of asthma, was completely cured by his residence on the ostrich farms; and a troublesome remittent fever, caught in the West Indies, from which I had suffered, off and on, during seven years, left me entirely from the time we went to live at Swaylands. There seems, indeed, to be much of truth in the boastful assertion one so often hears, "No one is ever ill here!" and the wonder is, not that doctors are so sparsely distributed throughout the Karroo, but that they ever think it worth while to settle there at all. People live quite contentedly two or more days' drive from the nearest doctor — medical help from Port Elizabeth being equally, if not more, inaccessible, owing to the fact that the train does not run every day—and from year's end to year's end they not only are never ill, but seem also quite exempt from the usual accidents which in other parts of the world are apt to befall humanity. They go out shooting, and their horses buck them off— a trifling, everyday event which is taken as a matter of course; they gallop recklessly across the *veldt*, over ground so full of treacherous holes that a horse is liable at any moment to get a sudden and ugly fall— indeed, he often does, but the colonist always rises unhurt; they drive home late at night along the roughest of roads, at a furious pace—often after imbibing far more than is usually conducive to safety— and their Cape carts or American spiders very naturally tumble into sluits, run into wire fences, perform somer-

F

saults down steep banks, and go through other startling acrobatic feats, all with perfect impunity to the occupants. No legs, arms, or ribs, to say nothing of necks, are ever broken.

And when the young colonist makes his first appearance on this world's stage, his advent is not made the occasion for any undue display of fuss or anxiety. It is not thought worth while to summon the doctor from his distant abode; some old Dutch or Hottentot woman, who has been a grandmother so often that her experience is large, is called in, and all goes well. The young colonist himself is invariably a flourishing specimen of humanity; the childish ailments to which so many of his less robust European contemporaries succumb, cause him no trouble, and, if indeed they attack him at all, he weathers them triumphantly. He thrives in the pure fresh air, revels in the healthy out-door life, eats, of course, to an enormous and alarming extent, and grows up a young giant. He enjoys the same immunity from accident as his elders, passing safely through even more "hair-breadth 'scapes" than they; his sturdy, independent spirit makes him equal to any emergency, and enables him, in whatever circumstances of difficulty or danger he may be placed, to take very good care of himself.

On the farm next to ours a tiny boy of three, while playing with the windlass of a deep well, and hanging on to the rope, suddenly let himself down with a run into the water. He was not much disconcerted, however; but, with wonderful presence of mind for such a baby, managed to get his feet firmly on the bucket, and finding the length of the rope just, though *only* just, allowed his mouth to come above the surface, remained immovable, roaring steadily and lustily till assistance came.

The long droughts are certainly very trying; indeed they could not possibly be endured by any country less wonderfully fertile than South Africa, where it is calculated that three good days' rain in the year, could we but have this regularly, would be sufficient to meet all the needs of the land. But often, for more than a year, there will be no rain worth mentioning; the dams, or large artificial reservoirs, of which each farm usually possesses several, gradually become dry; and the *veldt* daily loses more of its verdure, till at last all is one dull, ugly brown, and the whole plain lies parched and burnt up under a sky from which every atom of moisture seems to have departed—a hard, grey, metallic sky, as different as possible from the rich, deep-blue canopy which, far away to the north, spreads over lovely Algeria. The stock, with the pathetic tameness of thirst, come from all parts of the farm to congregate close round the house; the inquiring ostriches tapping with their bills on the windows as they look in at you, and the cattle lowing in piteous appeal for water; and you realize very vividly the force of such Scriptural expressions as, "the heaven was shut up," or, "a dry and thirsty land where no water is."

Then the hot winds sweep across the country,

making everybody tired, languid, head-achy and cross. Indeed, excessive irritability seems to be the general result of hot winds in all parts of the world; in Egypt, for instance, there is never so much crime among the natives as while the *khamseen* is blowing; every outbreak of the Arabs in Algiers invariably occurs during an extra bad sirocco; and in a Spanish family I knew in Havana there obtained a very sensible rule, unanimously adopted to avoid collisions of temper, *i.e.*, on the days of an especially venomous hot wind peculiar to Cuba an unbroken silence was maintained; no member of the family, on any pretence whatever, speaking to another. Even our pets were sulky on a hot wind day; and as for the ostriches, they were deplorable objects indeed as they stood gasping for breath, with pendent wings, open bills, and inflated throats, the pictures of imbecile dejection. In fact, everything human, four-footed, and feathered, in the whole Karroo, was as thoroughly unhappy as it could well be; with the sole exception of myself. My spirits, instead of falling below zero, would always rise in proportion as the surrounding air became more like the breath of a furnace; this was not owing, as may perhaps be supposed, to the possession of so rare a sweetness of temper as to render me happy under even the most adverse circumstances, but simply to a real and intense enjoyment of that weather which everyone else hated. While T——, closing every door and window as tightly as possible (which, however, is not saying much), would retire to his bath, there to spend a couple of hours in company

OSTRICHES IN A HOT WIND.

with books, papers, and numberless lemon-squashes, if lemons happened to be attainable; I would carry my chair outside, and, as I darned socks or repaired the latest trap-doors torn in our garments by the thorns, would revel in *my* bath of hot, dry air.

The dust which the hot wind brings with it is, however, a nuisance. There is more than enough dust at the best of times; and the difficulties—already considerable—of keeping a Karroo house neat and clean, are not lessened by the fact that, ten minutes after a careful progress round the room with that most perfect of dusters, a bunch of ostrich-feathers, you can distinctly sign your name with your finger on the little black writing-table, or make a drawing on the piano. But in a good hot wind you have far more than this average, everyday amount of "matter in the wrong place," and you eat and breathe dust.

Sometimes the wind carries the dust high up into the air, in straight, solid-looking columns rising from the ground just as a water-spout rises from the sea. An artist wishing to depict the pillar of the cloud going before the Israelites might well take the form of one of them as a model. Occasionally you see two or three of these columns wandering about the *veldt* in different directions; and woe betide the imperfectly-built house, or tall wind-mill pump, which has the ill-luck to stand in the path of one of these erratic visitants! We, alas! can speak from experience, our own "Stover" mill having been chosen as a victim and whirled aloft to its destruction! T——, while at Kimberley, in the early days of the diamond-fields, has often seen these dusty whirlwinds going about the camp, passing between the long rows of tents as if hesitating for a time which to attack; then suddenly "going for" one of them, causing instantaneous collapse and confusion.

Every Karroo house has a dam near it, and on a large farm there are generally three or four more of these reservoirs in different parts of the land. The selection of a suitable site for a dam requires some experience. An embankment is thrown up across a valley, where from the rising ground on either side the water is collected. The ground must be "brack," a peculiar kind of soil which, though loose and friable, is not porous. This brack is often used to cover the flat roofs of the houses; but unless it is well sifted and laid on thickly, dependence cannot always be placed on it, as *we* have several times found to our cost. Rows of willows or mimosas are generally planted along the banks of the dams; and though the moisture which is sucked up by their thirsty roots can ill be afforded, yet, in that most treeless of lands, their bright, fresh green is of immense value; and the poor ugly houses, standing so forlornly on the bare *veldt*, with but the narrowest and scantiest of gardens—if any—between them and the surrounding desert, seem redeemed from utter dreariness and desolation, and some slight look of home and of refinement is imparted by the dam's semicircle of trees. A good-sized dam is sometimes half a mile broad, and, when just filled after a good thunder-shower, is quite an imposing sheet of water. Occasionally, in very heavy thunder-storms, the glorious supplies pour in too lavishly; the embankment, unable to resist the pressure, gives way; and the disappointed farmer, who has ridden up in the hope of feasting his eyes on watery wealth, beholds his treasure flowing uselessly and aimlessly away across the *veldt*.

Then, too, even the noblest of dams *must* dry up in a long drought; and that landowner is wise who does not depend solely on this form of water-supply, but who takes the precaution of sinking one or more good wells. This is expensive work—especially when, as in our case, the hard rock has to be blown away by dynamite; a party of navvies, encamped on the farm for weeks, progressing but slowly and laboriously at the rate of about one foot per day, for which the payment is £5 a foot; but the advantage is seen during the protracted droughts. Then, on farms which only possess dams, the ostriches and other stock are seen lying dead in all directions, a most melancholy sight. Where there is a well, however, the animals can always be kept alive. The water may go down rather low, and the supply doled out to the thirsty creatures may not be very plentiful; but with careful management no stock need be lost during the longest of droughts. But, even with our good well, we found it necessary to be very economical; and the few small eucalypti and other trees which, with great difficulty, we kept alive near the house, have often for weeks together been obliged to content themselves with the soapy water from the baths; while our poor little patch of kitchen-garden has more than once had to be sacrificed and allowed to dry up—the water necessary for its irrigation being more than we could venture to spare.

In some parts of the country the inhabitants are occasionally in terrible straits for want of water; and during one severe drought some passing strangers, who rested a few hours at our house, told us a horrid story of how, at one of the "cantines" (combinations of inn and general store) along their road, they had asked for water to wash their hands, and a scanty supply was brought, with the request that no soap might be used, that same water being ultimately destined to make the tea! It sounds incredible, but I fear it is more likely to be truth than fiction, for the Dutch at the Cape are dirty enough for anything.

The partiality of the thunder-storms is surprising; sometimes one farm will have all its dams filled, while another near it does not get a drop of rain. Often, during a whole season, the thunder-clouds will follow the same course; one unlucky place being repeatedly left out. Swaylands was once for months passed over in this manner; our neighbours on both sides having an abundance of water, while we, like the unhappy little pig of nursery fame, "had none," and found it difficult to restrain envy, hatred, and malice.

Then, too, the clouds have such a deceitful and tantalizing way of collecting in magnificent masses, and coming rolling grandly up as if they really meant business at last—only to disperse quietly in a few hours, disappointing all the hopes they have raised.

Again and again you are deluded into believing the long, weary drought is indeed nearing its end; you feel so sure there is a tremendous rain just at hand, that you prepare for action, and, doubting the trustworthiness of those portions of the roof covered with brack, are careful to remove from beneath them everything liable to be spoilt by wet; then, having set your house in order, you wait eagerly to hear the first pattering of the longed-for drops. They do not come, however; it all ends in nothing, and soon every cloud is gone, and the sun blazes out once more in pitiless splendour.

Then at last, after "Wolf!" has been cried so often that you are off your guard, and—obstinately refusing to be taken in by the promising bank of clouds you noticed in the evening—have gone off to bed, expecting your waking eyes to rest only on the usual hard, hot, grey-blue sky—suddenly, in the middle of the night, you are aroused by a deafening noise, and your first confused, half-dreaming thought is that somehow or other you have got underneath the Falls of Niagara—house and all. Then a blue flash wakes you quite up, a terrific roar of thunder shakes the house, and you realize that what for months you have been so longing for has come at last! But there are penalties to be paid for it; and an ominous sound of trickling strikes your ear. Your bedroom unfortunately has a brack roof; and through the defective places in the latter, which every moment become larger and more numerous, streams of water are pouring in, till at last the room seems to be one large shower-bath. You think with horror of the books, writing-case, photographs, lace-trimmed hat, work-basket, boots, etc., all left in various exposed positions about the room, and—most frightful thought of all—of the coats and dresses hanging on the row of pegs in that corner where, to judge by the sound, the most substantial of all the cataracts seems to be descending; and you feel that you *must* learn at once the extent of your misfortune, and rescue what you can. You try to light a candle; but a well-directed jet of water has been steadily playing straight down into the candlestick, and a vicious sputter is the only response to your efforts. You are still struggling with the candle; trying to wipe it dry, using persuasive language to it, and as far from getting a light as ever; when your breath is suddenly taken away by a stream of ice-cold water pouring over your back, and you find that you have shipped as fine a "sea" as ever dashed through an incautiously-opened port. The flat roof, which has been collecting water till it has become like a tank, has given way under the pressure, and a wide crack has opened just above your head. Of course you are wet through, so is the bed on which you are sitting; and you make a prompt descent from the latter, only to find the floor one vast, shallow bath, in which your slippers are floating.

And now, as you grope about, hurriedly collecting the more perishable articles, and flinging them into the safety of the next room—which has a corrugated iron roof—you hear a dull roar; far off at first, but advancing nearer and nearer; till at last a grand volume of sound thunders past, and a broad, tossing river, impetuous as any mountain torrent, is suddenly at your very gates. It is the *sluit* coming down; filling, and perhaps widely overflowing, its deep channel, which, straight and steep as a railway cutting, has stood dry so long. In all directions these *sluits* are now careering over the country; and though occasionally their wild rush does some mischief, such as washing away ostriches' nests, drowning stock, or carrying into a dam such an accumulation of soil as to fill it up and render it useless— still, on the whole, the *sluit* is a most beneficent friend to the farmer. And now, at the first welcome sound of that friend's approach, you hear overhead the loud congratulations of the gentlemen, who, attired in ulsters, are hard at work on the roof, whither they have hastily scrambled to lessen as far as possible the deluge within. "This is worth £200 to us!" you hear in triumphant tones. "We're all right now for six months!" Then—less joyfully—comes a query as to how the great dam in the upper camp, which on a former sad occasion has "gone," will stand this time; but the general opinion is that, with the considerable strengthening it has since received, it will weather the storm; and in the meanwhile souls must be possessed in patience till the morning. And still the rain keeps on, steadily and noisily; and with all the discomfort, and with all the mischief it has wrought indoors, how thankful one is for it! And how one's heart is gladdened by that "sound of abundance of rain," and "voice of many waters!" It means everything to the farmer; the long drought over at last, the dams full, the parched country revived, the poor thin cattle no longer in danger of starvation; healthier ostriches, a better quality of feathers, a near prospect of nests, and in fact the removal of a load of cares and anxieties.

How early we are all astir on the morning after a big rain! and with what eager excitement we look out, in the first gleam of daylight, for that most welcome sight, the newly-filled dam! A wonderful transformation has indeed been worked in the appearance of things since last night. That unsightly dry bed of light-coloured soil, baked by the hot sun to the hardness of pottery, and broken up by a thousand intersecting deep cracks and fissures, which has so long been the ugliest feature among all our unpicturesque surroundings, offends the eye no more; and in its place there now lies in the early morning light a beautiful broad sheet of water, into which the yellow *sluit*, a miniature Niagara Rapids, is still lavishly pouring its wealth—not for many hours indeed will the impetuous course of this and numerous other *sluits*, large and small, begin gradually to subside. Everywhere the water is standing in immense pools and ponds; how to feed one unlucky pair of breeding-birds —my special charges—in a low-lying camp on the other side of the sluit is a problem which for the present I do not attempt to solve; indeed, to walk a yard from the door, even in the thickest of boots and shabbiest of garments, requires some courage, for it is anything but an easy matter to keep your feet, and if you fell, you would go into a perfect bath of mud. In some places lie accumulations of hailstones (accounting for the icy coldness of that impromptu shower-bath), and, though partially melted, some of them are still of the size of hazel nuts. The rain is over; and the friendly clouds to which we owe so much are already far off, and lie in white, round, solid-looking masses along the horizon. The sky, as if softened by its tempest of passion, seems of a bluer and more tender tint than it has been for a long time, and all nature appears full of joy and thanksgiving. From all sides you hear the loud chorus of myriads of rejoicing frogs, all croaking congratulations to each other, and all talking at once; they seem to have sprung suddenly into existence since last night, and their noise, discordant as it is, is not unwelcome after the long silence of the drought.

Toto, the instant he catches sight of the water, rushes out of the house, gallops wildly down to the dam, and plunges in, to swim round and round and round, barking with delight. He seems as if he could not have enough of the water; for when, after a long time, he has come out, and is on his way back to us, he suddenly changes his mind, and dashes back for another bathe. Then he seems to lose his head altogether, and vents his wild spirits in a sort of frenzied war-dance along the banks of the dam; seriously upsetting the composure, as well as the dignity, of the crow Bobby, a bird of neat and cleanly habits, who, long debarred from any more satisfactory bath than a washing-basin, has walked down, with the air of an explorer, to this new lake he has just discovered; and is croaking softly and contentedly to himself as he splashes the bright drops again and again over his dusty black plumage. He does not like Toto; indeed, there is a mutual jealousy between these two favoured pets of ours, and they are always rather glad of an excuse for a good row, such as now ensues.

When the commotion has subsided, and Toto is at a safe distance from the dam, a troop of ostriches come down to drink. They are no doubt delighted to find such an abundant supply of water, after the somewhat scanty allowance which has been portioned out to them of late; and they stand greedily scooping up large quantities with their broad bills; then assuming comical attitudes as they stretch out their distended necks to allow the fluid to run down. In the distance, about a dozen other ostriches are spreading their white wings and waltzing along magnificently—a pretty way of expressing their satisfaction at this new and delightful change in their circumstances. But it is sometimes an expensive amusement; and we feel relieved when all have settled down, with unbroken legs, into a more sober mood.

The fowls alone do not participate in the general rejoicing; their house was even less water-tight than our room, and they all seem to have caught cold, and look draggled and miserable. Two poor sitting-hens have been washed out of their nests in the kraal hedge;

their eggs are under water, and they wander about clucking despondently. By-and-by they will all be happier, when the waters have subsided a little, and they can pick succulent insects out of the softened ground; but in the meanwhile they show plainly that they do not see the good of living in a half-drowned world.

And here come two of the horses, with "September,"* one of our Kaffir herds, who has been out on the *veldt* to find and catch them. Like most of the other colonists, we have no stables, and when our animals have done their day's work, we let them go, unless an early start has to be made in the morning; then, as they sometimes go long distances, and are not to be caught in a hurry, those that will be wanted are kept in the kraal over-night. During severe droughts the horses are fed at the house; but when there is plenty of vegetation on the *veldt*, they pick up a living for themselves. They do not get very fat, nor are they handsome to look at; and if an English coachman could see their bony frames and rough, ungroomed coats, he would no doubt be filled with the profoundest contempt. Yet, with all their uncouth appearance, they are far more serviceable than his fat, sleek, overfed animals. They can travel much longer distances; they do not have such frequent colds and other ailments—lameness especially is quite unknown among them—and their services are always at the command of their master, of any of his friends and acquaintances, or

* Many of the negroes on Cape farms are named after the months.

even of perfect strangers who may happen to require a mount or a lift. For the colonist is as hospitable with his horses and his vehicles as he is with everything else that he possesses; and the arrival of an invited guest in a hired conveyance, though no unfrequent event at English country homes, is a thing quite unheard-of on Cape farms.

Although in many parts of South Africa horses do not require shoeing at all, they need it in the Karroo, where the ground is particularly stony. When a horse's shoes are worn out, he is worked for some time unshod, until the hoof, which had grown considerably, has worn down, and the animal begins to be a little tender-footed; then fresh shoes are put on. This plan renders it unnecessary for the blacksmith to use his knife, and ensures that the hoof is worn evenly; thus avoiding the lameness which in England is so often caused by the hoof not being pared straight.

And in the meanwhile the two horses have been saddled, and off go T—— and Mr. B—— on a tour of inspection round the farm; first of all making a bee-line for the opposite range of hills, where lies that particular dam in the fate of which we are so deeply interested. I cannot ride with them, much as I should have liked it; for the scenes of devastation indoors claim my attention, and with my dark-skinned handmaiden and another Kaffir woman, wife of one of the herds, whom I have pressed into the service, I go to work; boldly attacking first the most herculean task of all, *i.e.*, the cleaning of the bedroom out of which we were washed last night. Truly an Augean stable is this first room; and the sight of its horrors by daylight makes me wonder how by any possibility it can ever again be fit for human habitation. The water with which the bed has been deluged was no clear crystal stream—far from it—and pillows, sheets, and counterpane are of a rich brown hue; so are the toilet table and the once pretty window-curtains of blue-and-white Madras muslin, which now look melancholy indeed as they hang down, straight and limp, from their cornice. In fact, hardly anything in the room can boast of having remained perfectly dry and clean; and the floor is a pool of dirty water several inches deep. It all looks hopeless; but we refuse to be daunted, and set to work with a will; things dry quickly in such a sun as is now shining brightly outside; the mud is "clean" mud, too, and does not stain or spoil so irretrievably as that of most other places. A Falstaffian bundle is made up for the wash, which will keep a Kaffir hard at work for two good days turning the washing-machine; a vigorous scrubbing and "swabbing of decks" goes on indoors; and by the time the gentlemen return to lunch, in the best of spirits, and reporting the dam safe and splendidly full, things have already assumed a brighter aspect. T—— spends the afternoon in repairing the roof, and I walk about the house with a long broom, p⁁king and tapping the ceilings to indicate to him the ⁁ .ective spots; he does the work far better than it as originally done by the builder of the house, and never afterwards do we have so bad a deluge.

It was, however, very nearly equalled in magnitude by a previous one, which, while we were living at Hume Cottage, gave me the first experience of a big rain—and of a *brack* roof. T—— being away for a few days, I was alone in the house with my one black servant, who of course slept placidly through all the tumult of the elements. I, on the contrary—the bedroom being water-tight—was lying awake, listening and rejoicing as I thought of all the good this splendid rain would do us. Little did I suspect what it *was* doing in the sitting-room; and I cheerfully and briskly opened the door of the latter next morning, all unprepared for the sight which met my eyes. Poor little room! only a few days before we had taken such pride and pleasure in beautifying it—and now! It looked like nothing but the saloon of a steamer which had gone down and been fished up again. The treacherous roof had let in floods of dirty brown water in all directions; the Turkish rugs were half buried in mud; the new bent-wood chairs looked like neglected old garden seats which for years had braved all weathers; and the table-cloth, on the artistic colours of which we had prided ourselves, gave a very good idea of the probable state of Sir Walter Raleigh's cloak after serving as an impromptu carpet for his queen. But the brunt of the storm had fallen on two sets of hanging bookshelves, well filled with nicely-bound volumes, and gracefully draped with some of our pet pieces of Turkish needlework. The books all looked as if they had been boiled; and the colour which had come out of their swollen and pulpy bindings had run down the saturated embroideries in long streaks, showing where a red book had stood, where a blue or green one, etc. Fortunately, a good cleaning and washing restored most things to a tidy, if not perfectly fresh appearance; but those poor books never recovered.

In a few days—incredibly few—the effects of a good rain are seen in the appearance of the *veldt*, which rapidly loses its dry, burnt-up look. But, even before the perennial bush has had time to recover its succulence and verdure, all the spaces between its isolated tufts are covered with the softest and most delicate-looking vegetation, which, as if by magic, has sprung suddenly into existence. All these plants, which are of many different kinds, and some of which possess very minute and pretty flowers, are indiscriminately called by the Dutch *opslaag* (" that which comes up "); and if you happen at the time of their appearance to have a troop of infant ostriches, there is no better food for the little creatures than this tender, bright-green foliage. They are but short-lived little plants; the hot sun soon drying them up.

If the Cape Colony only possessed mountains high enough to give an abundant rainfall, what a gloriously fertile country it would be! Without droughts, what a splendid possession our farm would be to us! Often, when the coveted clouds have passed so close that it seemed as if they must be just about to break over the farm, T——, remembering how the firing of the great guns at Woolwich sometimes brings down the rain, has thought it might be a good plan to send up a fire-balloon with a charge of dynamite, and, catching the rain on our land, prevent it from going off so disappointingly elsewhere.

The short Cape winter, corresponding in duration to the English summer, is never severe. Cold winds blow from the direction of Graaff-Reinet on the not very frequent occasions when the higher mountains round that little town are for a short time topped with snow. In June and July the evenings and early mornings are decidedly cold. There is sometimes a little frost at night, and fires are pleasant; but in the middle of the day there is always warm, bright sunshine. Altogether, our winter under the Southern Cross has nothing cheerless or depressing about it; and those to whom the heat of the long summer has been a little trying, find the change most bracing and invigorating.

For farm life in the Karroo much the same kind of clothing is required as in England; everything must of course be of good strong material, and black or very dark colours are, in that dustiest of lands, to be avoided. Ladies' washing dresses should not be too delicate, nor should they be such as to require elaborate getting up; for of all the numerous things which on our isolated farms have to be done—either well, badly, or indifferently—at home, the laundry department is the very furthest from being our *forte*. The clothes become so discoloured from being continually washed in the yellow water of the dams; and the Kaffir women —if they profess to starch and iron at all—do it so badly, that the things are often unwearable. As for myself, I was fortunate in possessing for everyday wear strong cotton dresses of Egyptian manufacture; which required neither starching nor ironing, and, after being washed, and dried in the sun, were ready to be put on at once. For driving, and especially for the long journeys of several days, which sometimes have to be taken in Cape carts or spiders, a light dust-cloak is indispensable. Boots and shoes, more than anything else, need to be strong, and for gentlemen who live the active outdoor life of the farms, there is nothing so serviceable as the country-made *veldtschoon*.

CHAPTER VI.

OSTRICHES.

An unwilling ride—First sight of an ostrich farm—Ridiculous mistakes about ostriches—Decreased value of birds and feathers—Chicks—Plumage of ostriches—A frightened ostrich—The plucking-box—Sorting feathers—Voice of the ostrich—Savage birds—" Not afraid of a dicky-bird ! "—Quelling an ostrich—Birds killed by men in self-defence—Nests—An undutiful hen—Darby and Joan—A disconsolate widower—A hen-pecked husband—Too much zeal—Jackie—Cooling the eggs—The white-necked crow—Poisoning jackals—Ostrich eggs in the kitchen—A quaint old writer on ostriches—A suppliant bird—Nest destroyed by enraged ostrich—An old bachelor.

A FEW years before my marriage, having, as usual, fled the terrors of the English winter, I was with a friend in Egypt. And one morning this friend and I stood in the court of the Hôtel du Nil in Cairo ; preparing to mount donkeys and start on a photographing expedition to Heliopolis (the " On " of the Scriptures), and Matariyeh, one of the supposed resting-places of the Holy Family on their flight into Egypt. The fussy, bustling little German manager of the hotel, with his usual paternal care for his guests, was commending us, in a long and voluble Arabic speech, to the special care and attention of the donkey-boys ; with numerous minute instructions, all unintelligible to us, as to our route, etc. Then, just as we had mounted, he turned to us and said, " I have told them to show you something more on the way back, something *very interesting.*" " What is it ? " we were about to ask ; but before we could get the words out, the ubiquitous little man had bustled off to other business ; and we ourselves were flying at a headlong pace down the narrow Arab street, closely pursued by our impetuous donkey-boys ; who, anxious to make an imposing start, urged on our animals, not only with savage yells and blows, but also with frequent and cruel digs from the sharp points of our camera's tripod stand.

Even after we had left the town far behind us, and our tyrants, for lack of an admiring crowd before whom to exhibit us, allowed us to settle down into a peaceful trot, it was quite useless to look to them for any information concerning this promised interesting sight ; for our few words of Algerian Arabic did not avail in Egypt ; and as for the European vocabulary of the donkey-boys, it was, as usual, strictly limited to an accurate knowledge of all the bad words in English, French and German. N.B.—A donkey-boy is never promoted to the dignity of being called a donkey-*man*, but, however old and grey he may have grown in the service, always retains the juvenile appellation.

On arriving at Heliopolis, our ungratified curiosity was soon forgotten in the interest of seeing that venerable obelisk which once, in all probability, looked down on the wedding procession of Joseph and the daughter of "Potipherah, priest of On;" and the sun gave us some good pictures of that sole remaining relic of the city where he himself was formerly worshipped. We spent a long morning at Heliopolis and Matariyeh; and it was not until we had proceeded some distance along the dusty road leading back to Cairo, that we suddenly recollected there was yet one more sight on our programme. The sun was blazing down fiercely on us; we were very tired; longing visions of the Hôtel du Nil luncheon, the hour for which had already come, filled our minds; and most devoutly did we hope the donkey-boys might forget they had something more to show us, and—possibly being hungry themselves—take us straight home. But no! suddenly our reluctant donkeys were abruptly turned from the homeward course on which they were trotting so merrily; and by main force pushed into a particularly uninviting path branching off at right angles from the road. We made one desperate effort to turn them back; but our tormentors flew to their heads, and, dragging, pushing, almost lifting them along, applied the tripod's spikes with fresh energy. In vain did we expostulate; explaining piteously, with all the powers of pantomime at our command, that we were tired and hungry, and wanted to go back to the hotel; that we would come and see this interesting sight, whatever it was, tomorrow, *bookra*—that favourite word of the procrastinating Orientals, which, like the *mañana* of the Spaniards, soon becomes hatefully familiar from constant hearing, and which is second only to the terrible *baksheesh!* The relentless donkey-boys, beyond chuckling over our disappointment, took no notice whatever of our appeals; and on we had to go at a rapid gallop, stirring up dense clouds of the blinding, choking, evil-smelling Egyptian dust; and realizing, as did Mark Twain when ascending the Pyramid, how powerless one is in the hands of Arabs, who surely, with such iron wills, ought to be good mesmerists. Resigning ourselves at last to our fate with the patience of despair, we tried, though with but languid interest, to find out what we were going to see; but for a long time could get nothing intelligible from the donkey-boys, who only enjoyed our mystification. At last one of them, struck by a bright idea, pointed to J——'s hat, in which was an ostrich-feather; and we guessed at once that the Khedive's ostrich farm, which we knew was somewhere in the neighbourhood of Cairo, was the object of our unwilling ride. Here was another disappointment! Not even a ruined mosque, picturesque Arab house, or other possible subject for the camera, to reward us for our fatigue and discomfort; nothing but dry, barren-looking land, ugly modern European buildings, and ungainly birds! We walked hurriedly, and with great indifference, past the rows of camps, each with its pair of breeding-birds; felt little regret on being denied entrance to the incubator-rooms, which, happening to contain young chicks, were closed to the public; and rejoiced exceedingly when, our task done, and our tyrants appeased by our complete subjugation, we were at last on our way back to Cairo.

Thus, in weariness and indifference, I viewed an ostrich farm for the first time. Could I but have had one vision of the happy home, situated among just such surroundings, which awaited me in the future, with what different eyes would I have looked on all the minutest details of a daily life destined one day to be mine! How eagerly would I have bribed the custodian of the incubators for just one peep at the little rough-coated baby ostriches, if I had known what numbers of these comical wee things were in future to be my carefully-tended nurslings! And when T——, anxious to compare notes, sometimes asks me how this or that was managed on the Khedive's farm, and I am unable to give accurate information, I still regret that lost opportunity; and blush at the remembrance of the base longing for luncheon, to which, I fear, the want of observation was chiefly due.

It is rather surprising to find how little is known in England about ostrich-farming. Any information on the subject seems quite new to the hearers; and the strangest questions are sometimes asked—as, for instance, whether ostriches fly; whether they bite; whether we ever ride or drive them, etc. It is always taken for granted that a vicious bird administers his kick backwards, like a horse; and there seems still to be a very general belief in those old popular errors of which the natural history of these creatures possesses more than the average share. If you look at the picture of an ostrich, you will be sure to find, in nine cases out of ten, that the drawing is ludicrously incorrect; the bird being almost invariably represented with three toes instead of two; and with a tail consisting of a large and magnificent bunch of *wing*-feathers, the finest and longest of "prime whites." Farmers would only be too thankful if their birds *had* such tails, instead of the short, stiff, scrubby tuft of inferior feathers which in reality forms the caudal appendage.

Each of my friends and relatives, when first told, at the time of our engagement, that T—— was "an ostrich-farmer," received the intelligence with an amused smile; and the clergyman at whose church we were married seemed quite taken aback on obtaining so novel and unexpected an answer to his question, during the vestry formalities, as to T——'s vocation in life. He hesitated, pen in hand, for some time; made T—— repeat and explain the puzzling word; and at last only with evident reluctance inscribed it in the church books.

In the early days of ostrich-farming splendid fortunes were made. Then, feathers were worth £100 per lb., the plumes of one bird at a single plucking realizing on an average £25. For a good pair of breeding-birds £400, or even £500, was no uncommon price; and little chicks, only just out of the egg, were worth £10 each. Indeed, the unhatched eggs have sometimes been valued at the same amount. But, since the supply has become so much greater than the demand, things are sadly changed for the farmers; our best pair of ostriches would not now sell for more than £12, and experience has taught us to look for no higher sum than thirty shillings for the feathers of the handsomest bird at one plucking. At the same time, if a lady wishes to buy a good feather in London or Paris, she has to pay nearly the same price as in former times.*

There are not many young animals prettier than a little ostrich-chick during the first few weeks of life. It has such a sweet, innocent baby-face, such large eyes, and such a plump, round little body. All its movements are comical, and there is an air of conceit and independence about the tiny creature which is most amusing. Instead of feathers, it has a little rough coat which seems all made up of narrow strips of material, of as many different shades of brown and grey as there are in a tailor's pattern-book, mixed with shreds of black; while the head and neck are apparently covered with the softest plush, striped and coloured just like a tiger's skin on a small scale. On the whole, the little fellow, on his first appearance in the world, is not unlike a hedgehog on two legs, with a long neck.

One would like these delightful little creatures to remain babies much longer than they do; but they grow quickly, and with their growth they soon lose all their prettiness and roundness; their bodies become angular and ill-proportioned, a crop of coarse, wiry feathers sprouts from the parti-coloured strips which formed their baby-clothes, and they enter on an ugly "hobbledehoy" stage, in which they remain for two or three years.

* Although, since these pages were written, ostriches have somewhat increased in value it cannot, of course, be expected that they will ever again command the prices of former days.

OSTRICH-CHICKS.

A young ostrich's rough, bristly, untidy-looking "chicken-feathers" are plucked for the first time when he is nine months old; they are stiff and narrow, with very pointed tips, and their ugly appearance gives no promise of future beauty. They do not look as if they could be used for anything but making feather brooms. In the second year they are rather more like what ostrich-feathers ought to be, though still very narrow and pointed; and not until their wearer is plucked for the third time have they attained their full width and softness.

During the first two years the sexes cannot be distinguished, the plumage of all being of a dingy drab mixed with black; the latter hue then begins to predominate more and more in the male bird with each successive moulting, until at length no drab feathers are left. At five years the bird has attained maturity; the plumage of the male is then of a beautiful glossy black, and that of the female of a soft grey, both having white wings and tails. In each wing there are twenty-four long white feathers, which, when the wing is spread out, hang gracefully round the bird like a lovely deep fringe—just as I have sometimes in Brazilian forests, seen fringes of large and delicate fern-fronds hanging, high overhead, from the branches of some giant tree.

The ostrich's body is literally "a bag of bones;" and the enormously-developed thighs, which are the only fleshy part of the bird, are quite bare, their coarse skin being of a peculiarly ugly blue-grey colour. The little flat head, much too small for the huge body, is also bald, with the exception of a few stiff bristles and scanty tufts of down; such as also redeem the neck from absolute bareness. During the breeding season the bill of the male bird, and the large scales on the fore part of his legs, assume a beautiful deep rose-colour, looking just as if they were made of the finest pink coral; in some cases the skin of the head and neck also becomes red at that time.

The North African or Barbary ostriches, several of which are to be seen at the Jardin d'Essai, in Algiers, have bright red thighs, head, and neck, and are altogether far handsomer than the Cape birds; their feathers also, being larger, softer, and possessing longer filaments, command much higher prices than those of their southern brethren.

Altogether, ostriches are queer-looking creatures; they are so awkward, so out of proportion, and everything about them, with the exception of their plumage and their big, soft, dark eyes, is so quaintly ugly as to suggest the idea that they have only by some mistake survived the Deluge, and that they would be more in their right place embedded in the fossiliferous strata of the earth than running about on its surface. And how they *do* run! Only startle an ostrich; and very little is sufficient to do this, his nerves being of the feeblest, and "his heart in his mouth" at even the smallest or most imaginary danger. What a jump he gives, and what a swerve to one side! Surely it must have dislocated some of his joints. But no; off he goes, flinging out his clumsy legs, and twisting himself about as he runs, till you almost expect to see him come to pieces, or, at any rate, fling off a leg, as a lobster casts a claw, or a frightened lizard parts from its tail. An ostrich's joints seem to be all loose, like those of a lay-figure when not properly tightened up. He rapidly disappears from view; and the last you see of him he is, as Mark Twain has it, "still running"—apparently with no intention of stopping till he has reached the very centre of Africa. But his mad scamper will most probably end a few miles off, with a tumble into a wire fence, and a broken leg.

Sometimes, however, ostriches, when they take fright, run so long and get so far away that their owner never recovers them. One we heard of, to whose tail a mischievous boy had tied a newspaper, went off at railway speed, and no tidings of it were ever received. Once, when T—— was collecting his birds for plucking, one of them was unaccountably seized with a sudden panic, and bolted; and though T—— mounted at once and rode after it, he neither saw nor heard of it again.

On a large farm, when plucking is contemplated, it is anything but an easy matter to collect the birds—the gathering together of ours was generally a work of three days. Men have to be sent out in all directions to drive the birds up, by twos and threes, from the far-off spots to which they have wandered; little troops are gradually brought together, and collected, first in a large enclosure, then in a small one, the plucking-kraal, in which they are crowded together so closely, that the most savage bird has no room to make himself disagreeable.

Besides the gate through which the ostriches are driven into the kraal, there is an outlet at the opposite end, through the "plucking-box." This latter is a most useful invention, saving much time and trouble. It is a very solid wooden box, in which, though there is just room for an ostrich to stand, he cannot possibly turn round; nor can he kick, the sides of the box being too high. At each end there is a stout door; one opening inside, the other outside the kraal. Each bird in succession is dragged up to the first door, and, after more or less of a scuffle, is pushed in and the door slammed behind him. Then the two operators, standing one on each side of the box, have him completely in their power; and with a few rapid snips of their shears his splendid wings are soon denuded of their long white plumes. These, to prevent their tips from being spoilt, are always cut before the quills are ripe. The stumps of the latter are allowed to remain some two or three months longer, until they are so ripe that they can be pulled out—generally by the teeth of the Kaffirs—without hurting the bird. It is necessary to pull them; the feathers, which by their weight would have caused the stumps to fall out naturally at the right time, being gone. Some farmers, anxious to hurry on the next crop of feathers, are cruel enough to draw the stumps before they are ripe; but nature, as usual, resents the interference with her laws, and the feathers of birds which have been thus treated soon deteriorate. It is best to pluck only once a year. The tails, and the glossy black feathers on the bodies of the birds, having small quills, are not cut, but pulled out; this, everyone says, does not hurt the birds, but there is an unpleasant tearing sound about the operation, and I think it must make their eyes water.

After a plucking would come several very busy days of sorting and tying up the feathers in readiness for the market; for T——, whenever he could spare the time, preferred doing this work himself to employing the professional sorters in Port Elizabeth, who charge exorbitantly. During these few days everything had to give way to feathers, large piled-up masses of which crowded the rooms, till we seemed to be over head and ears in feathers. Feathers covered the floor and invaded every article of furniture, especially monopolizing the dining-table; and when, at all sorts of irregular hours, we grudgingly allowed ourselves time for rough, impromptu meals of cold or tinned meat, we picnicked among feathers. It was useless to attempt keeping the rooms either tidy or clean while sorting was going on; and we resigned ourselves to living for those two or three days in a state at which owners of neat English homes would shudder—indeed, those only who have seen the process of sorting can form any idea of the untidiness, the dust, the fluffs, and the sneezing. But they were pleasant days; and many an interesting book will always be associated in our minds with the sorting of ostrich-feathers; for, while T—— arranged prime whites, blacks, tails, feminas, chicken-feathers, etc., according to length, colour, and quality, I enlivened the monotony of his work by reading aloud.

Sometimes the white feathers would be dirty—for there is nothing an ostrich likes better than sitting down to cool himself in the muddiest dam he can find —then it was necessary to wash them, dip them into strong raw starch, and shake them in the hot sun, beating two bundles of them together till quite dry. The starch makes them look very pretty and fluffy; and young ladies in England who economically wash their own feathers would find it a great improvement. Ostrich-feathers are quite tabooed by ladies in South Africa; they are too common, every Kaffir or Hottentot wearing one in his dirty, battered hat.

If an ostrich-feather is held upright, its beautiful form—graceful as the frond-like branch of the cocoa-nut palm, which it somewhat resembles—is at once seen to be perfectly even and equal on both sides, its stem dividing it exactly in the centre; whereas the stems of other feathers are all more or less on one side. The ancient Egyptians, observant of this—as of everything in nature—chose the ostrich-feather as the sacred emblem of truth and justice, setting it upon the head of Thmei, goddess of truth.

After a good rain, ostriches soon begin to make nests; the males become very savage, and their note of defiance—*brooming*, as it is called by the Dutch—is heard in all directions. The bird inflates his neck in a cobra-like fashion, and gives utterance to three deep roars; the two first short and *staccato*, the third very prolonged. Lion-hunters all agree in asserting that the roar of the king of beasts and that of the most foolish of birds are identical in sound; with this difference only, that the latter, when near, resembles the former very far away. T——, when hunting in the interior, has often been deceived by the sound—expecting a lion, and finding only an ostrich.

When the birds are savage—*quei*, as the Dutch call it—they become very aggressive, and it is impossible to walk about the camps unless armed with a weapon of defence called a "tackey." This is simply a long and stout branch of mimosa, with the thorns all left on at the end. It seems but a feeble protection against a foe who, with one stroke of his immensely powerful leg, can easily kill a man; the kick, no less violent than that of a horse, being rendered infinitely more dangerous by the formidable claw with which the foot is armed. Those, however, who are well practised in the use of the tackey are able, with the coolness of Spanish bull-fighters, to stand and await the charge of the terrible assailant. They allow him to come to what, to the inexperienced eye, seem unpleasantly close quarters; then, just as he prepares to strike, the tackey is boldly thrust into his face. The thorns oblige him to close his eyes, and he can only run blindly forward; the bearer of the tackey springing on one side, and gaining time to proceed some distance on his way, before the silly bird has recovered from his bewilderment and makes a fresh charge, when the weapon is again presented.

Fortunately, you are never assailed by more than one ostrich at a time; for in the large camps of some two thousand acres each—in which the birds are not fenced off in pairs, but live almost in the freedom of wild creatures—each one has his own domain, separated from those of others by some imaginary boundary-line of his own, visible only to himself, but as clearly marked out as the beat of a London policeman. There, in company with one or perhaps two hens, he dwells monarch of all he surveys; any other ostrich daring to invade his territory is at once attacked; and the human intruder is closely followed, his tackey in constant requisition, until the feathered lord of the land has seen him safely off the premises. Immediately after thus speeding the parting guest, the most savage bird is quite harmless; he dismisses you from his thoughts, and walks quietly back, feeding as he goes. And in the distance you see the head and long neck of his neighbour, whose kingdom you have now entered, and whose sharp eyes spied you out the instant your foot crossed his frontier. *He* now advances towards you with jerky, spasmodic movements, as if he were bowing you a welcome; this, however, is far from his thoughts, and after sitting down once or twice to give you his challenge—whereby he hopes you will be intimidated—he trots up defiantly, and the tackey's services are again required. Thus, during a morning's walk through the camps, you may be escorted in succession by four or five vicious birds, all determined to have your life if possible, yet held completely in check by a few mimosa thorns.

When an ostrich challenges he sits down ; and, flapping each broad wing alternately, inflates his neck, and throws his head back, rolling it from side to side, and with each roll striking the back of his head against his bony body with so sharp and resounding a blow that a severe headache seems likely to be the result.

A person on horseback is even more obnoxious to the ostriches than a pedestrian; and a ride through the camps enables one to realize how true to life is the description, in the Book of Job, of a vicious bird: " What time she lifteth up herself on high, she scorneth the horse and his rider." The creature, when preparing for an attack, draws itself up, stands on tiptoe, stretches its neck to the full extent, and really seems to gain several feet in height. And, indeed, it does its best to knock you off your horse. T—— once saw a man riding as desperately as Tam O'Shanter, with an ostrich in close pursuit. It kept up with him, helping his horse along with an occasional well-placed kick; while the unhappy rider, hoping to intimidate his assailant, was again and again firing off his revolver into the air, but without effect.

As the new arrival in a country subject to earthquakes begins by thinking very lightly of these disturbances, but finds his appreciation of their importance increase with every successive shock; so the new chum in South Africa, inclined at first to look with contempt on the precautions taken against savage ostriches, learns in time to have a proper respect for the foolish, innocent-looking creatures, whose soft, dark-brown eyes look at him so mildly (when he is on the right side of the fence) that he finds it impossible to believe the stories told him of their wickedness, and nothing but a closer acquaintance can undeceive him. On one of the farms a sturdy new-comer, six feet in height, starting for an early morning walk, was cautioned against going into a certain camp where the ostriches were dangerous. He laughed at his friends' advice, told them he was "not afraid of a dicky-bird!" and—disdaining the proffered tackey—started off straightway in the forbidden direction. He did not return home to dinner; a search was made for him; and eventually he was found, perched up on a high ironstone boulder; just out of reach of a large ostrich, which was doing sentry, walking up and down, and keeping a vicious eye on him. There he had sat for hours, nearly roasted alive (ironstone boulders in the Karroo can get so hot in the sun that it blisters your hand to touch them); and there he would have had to sit till sundown, had not the timely appearance of his friends relieved him of the too-pressing attentions of the "dicky-bird."

Another gentleman had a theory that any creature, however savage, could be subdued—"quelled," as he said—by the human eye. One day he tried to quell one of his own ostriches; with the result that he was presently found by T—— in a very pitiable predicament, lying flat on the ground; while the subject of his experiment jumped up and down on him, occasionally varying the treatment by sitting on him.

T—— once bought an ostrich which had killed two men; and which, although an unusually fine bird, was, on account of its evil reputation, sold to him for a very low price. Ostriches appear to have a strong aversion to all the negro race. They attack Kaffirs and Hottentots much more readily than they do their white masters; and although—as has just been seen—they are very far from showing that amount of respect for the latter which is desirable, they seem—except during the breeding season—to stand in some sort of awe of a white man as compared with the "niggers," for whom they have the deepest contempt.

They are uncertain, too, and take sudden and unaccountable dislikes. One poor Kaffir woman, coming up to work at the house, was attacked, inside the gate, by one of the tame old ostriches, which—looking out for scraps thrown from the kitchen, stealing the fowls' food, or now and then picking up and swallowing a delicious piece of soap left for an unguarded moment on the washing-machine—prowled about round the house, and of which no one had ever dreamed of being afraid. Her solitary and scanty skirt, torn from the top to the bottom, showed how narrow had been her escape; and she looked livid under her dark skin, as she came in to ask me for needle and thread to repair the rent.

It has several times happened that one of our herds, in danger of his life, has been obliged, in self-defence, to kill a vicious ostrich; and, the finest and most promising birds—naturally the most savage—being invariably the victims, the loss is always a serious one.

It is indeed no small trial, when, perhaps just as you are comfortably seated at the breakfast table, the black face of " April," " August," or " September "—fraught with bad news, and looking very frightened and ashamed—is suddenly thrust in at the door; and, with much rolling of white eyeballs, a tragic tale is told, in the most dismal of voices, and with many harrowing details, of how "Red Wing" or "White Neck" was *quei*, and attacked the narrator up in the big camp; with the sad consequence that you are now *minus* one of the best birds on the farm. But the poor fellow cannot be blamed or fined for defending his life; orders are given to pluck and bring down the unfortunate bird's feathers—the last he will ever yield—and somehow a dead bird's plumes *always* seem the most beautiful—

> " And then to breakfast, with
> What appetite you have."

Toto, although in general no coward, could never, after a severe kick he received on first coming to the farm, be brought to face a savage bird. Collies can, however, be made very useful in collecting and driving ostriches; and Mr. Evans, of Rietfontein, one of our neighbours, had several which were perfectly trained; working as well with the birds as their relatives in Scotland and Wales do with sheep.

A few of our birds were fenced off in breeding-camps; each pair having a run of about one hundred acres. One of these camps was directly opposite the house; and from the windows we could observe the regularity with which the two birds, sitting alternately on the eggs, came on and off at their fixed times. The cock always takes his place upon the nest at sundown, and sits through the night—his dark plumage making him much less conspicuous than the light-coloured hen; with his superior strength and courage, too, he is a better defender of the nest against midnight marauders. At nine in the morning, with unfailing punctuality, the hen comes to relieve him, and take up her position for the day. At the end of the six weeks of sitting, both birds, faithfully as the task has been shared between them, are in a very enfeebled state, and miserably poor and thin.

One undutiful hen—having apparently imbibed advanced notions—absolutely refused to sit at all; and the poor husband, determined not to be disappointed of his little family, did all the work himself; sitting bravely and patiently day and night, though nearly dead with exhaustion, till the chicks were hatched out. The next time this pair of birds had a nest, the cock's mind was firmly made up that he would stand no more nonsense. He fought the hen; giving her so severe a thrashing that she was all but killed—and this Petruchio-like treatment had the desired effect, for the wife never again rebelled, but sat submissively.

Very different from this couple were the Darby and Joan in the camp opposite our windows. One unlucky morning the hen, frightened by a Kaffir's dog, ran into the wire fence, and was so terribly injured that she had to be killed. For two years poor Darby was a disconsolate widower, and all attempts to find him a satisfactory second wife were unavailing; several hens, which, soon after his loss, were in succession placed in his camp, being only rescued in time, and at the tackey's point, from being kicked to death. The bare idea of there being anything pathetic about an ostrich seems absurd—and indeed this is the only instance I have known of anything of the kind—but it was truly pitiful to watch this poor bird, as, day after day, and nearly all day long, he wandered up and down, up and down, the length of his camp, in the hard, beaten track worn by his restless feet along the side of the fence.

When his time of mourning at length came to an end, and poor Joan's long-vacant place was filled, we at first rejoiced. But we soon doubted whether, after all, he had not been happier as a widower. For the new wife, a magnificent hen, considerably above the average size, had him in complete subjection; his spirit seemed quite broken, probably with long fretting, and he made no attempt to hold his own, but was for the rest of his days the most hen-pecked—or ought I to say hen-*kicked?*—of husbands. Some amount of stratagem was even necessary on my part, to ensure that he had enough to eat (this pair of birds, being near the house, were under my special care, and during droughts were daily fed by me); for every time he came near the food, the greedy hen would persistently drive him away, standing on tiptoe and hissing viciously at him—and I soon saw that it was useless to attempt feeding them together. But the poor, ill-used old bird and I were good friends, and quite understood one another; and at all sorts of odd times—watching for those golden opportunities when his tyrant was safely out of sight at the further end of the camp—he would come down to the fence and look out for me, and I would bring him a good feed of mealies.

As a father, Darby was no less devoted than he had formerly been as a husband; and to please him we allowed his chicks to remain with him, and set the whole family free to roam where they liked about the *veldt;* breaking through the usual rule, which is to take the little birds from the parents when two or three days old, and herd them near the house. For they never become as tame when brought up by the old ones as when accustomed from the first to human society. These poor little birds, I am sorry to say, did not flourish under parental guardianship; indeed, it was not long before they were all dead. For their well-meaning, but over-zealous father, apparently thinking no *veldt* good enough for them, kept them continually on the move; and, in his perpetual search for "fresh woods and pastures new," took them such long distances that he literally walked them as well as himself to death. Not many days after the last chick's departure, Darby's own poor body, worn to a skeleton by these restless wanderings, following on six weeks of incubation, was found on the *veldt*.

When, as sometimes happens, one solitary chick is reared at the house, it becomes absurdly and often inconveniently tame. A friend of ours, on returning to his farm at the end of a severe thunderstorm, found that an ostrich's nest had been washed away. Some of the eggs were rescued from the water, and—being of course deserted by the parents—were placed in an incubator, where, contrary to all expectations, one chick came out. This bird, Jackie, became the tamest and most audacious of pets; and, like many another spoilt only child, was often a terrible nuisance. All the little niggers about the place had a lively dread of him; and he requisitioned their food in the boldest manner. As they sat on the ground at meals, with plates of boiled pumpkin and rice in their laps, he would come up, and, stretching his snake-like neck over their heads, or insinuating it under their arms, would coolly help himself to the contents of one plate after another. Occasionally he would make for the unhappy youngsters in so menacing a manner as to frighten them into dropping their plates altogether; then, while his victims ran away crying, he would squat on his heels among the *débris*, and regale his enormous appetite at leisure.

But one day retribution came. Being free of the kitchen—simply because no one could keep him out—he was not long in observing that the pumpkin and rice always came out of one particular pot; and, the idea suddenly occurring to him that he could do no better than go straight to the fountain-head for his favourite dish, he walked up, full of joyful anticipation, to the fire where this pot was bubbling. The cook—who, being mother to several of the ill-used children, did not love

Jackie—offered no friendly interference to save him from his fate; and, plunging his bill into the pot, he greedily scooped up, and, with the lightning-like rapidity of ostriches, tossed down his throat, a large mouthful of boiling rice. Poor fellow! the next moment he was dancing round the kitchen, writhing with agony, shaking his head nearly off, and twisting his neck as if bent on tying it in a knot. Finally he dashed wildly from the house; the cook, avenged at last for all the dinners he had devoured, called after him as he stumbled out at the door, "Serve you right, Jackie!"—and away he fled across the *veldt*, till the last that was seen of him was a little cloud of white dust vanishing on the horizon. He returned a sadder and a wiser bird; and it was long before he again ventured inside the kitchen.

When about a year old, Jackie was sold to a farmer who had long coveted him; and who, no doubt, soon repented of his purchase. He was now sufficiently strong to give a good hard kick; and, being a more daring freebooter than ever, and no respecter of persons, he would march up and attack any one he saw carrying food, or what he thought might be food; endeavouring, by a well-aimed blow, to strike it out of their hands; his evil design generally succeeding. At length his master, tired of hearing constant complaints of his conduct, and impatient of his perpetual intrusion indoors, tried putting him into a camp. There, however, he obstinately refused to remain. As soon as he was put in, he would squat down, laying his head and neck on the ground; then, making himself as flat as possible, he would "squirm" out, not without some difficulty, under the lowest wire of the fence. It was impossible to keep him in; and he was left to his own devices, calmly regarded as a necessary evil, and allowed to be as great a nuisance as he liked.

But poor Jackie soon ceased from troubling—his end, as may well be imagined, being brought about by no other cause than his own moral obliquity. One day he wandered down to the river, where some Kaffir women were washing clothes; their children, a group of little animated nude bronzes, playing near them. One little fellow, who was eating, was of course instantly spied out by the covetous Jackie; who rushed to kick him, but in so doing tumbled down in the rocky bed of the river, and broke his own leg. The inevitable result followed, and Jackie, like all other broken-legged ostriches, had to be killed.

The hen ostrich lays every alternate day; and if, for each egg laid, one is taken from the nest, she will continue laying until she has produced from twenty to thirty. One, which belonged to T——, laid sixty eggs without intermission. If no eggs are taken away, the hen leaves off laying as soon as she has from fifteen to twenty; the latter being the greatest number that can be satisfactorily covered by the birds. The surplus eggs are placed in incubators. It is best not to give much artificial food to the birds while sitting; as, if overfed, they become restless, and are liable to desert the nest.

Every morning and evening the nest, or rather the

shallow indentation in the sandy ground which forms this simplest of all "homes without hands," is left uncovered for a quarter of an hour, to allow the eggs to cool. The sight of nests thus apparently deserted has probably given rise to the erroneous idea that the ostrich leaves her eggs to hatch in the sun. The passage in the book of Job: "Which leaveth her eggs in the earth, and warmeth them in the dust," is also generally supposed to point to the same conclusion, though in reality there can be no doubt that the latter part of the sentence simply applies to the warming of the eggs by the heat of the bird's body as she sits over them in her dusty nest. Stupid though she is, she has more sense than to believe in the possibility of the sun hatching her eggs; she is indeed quite aware of the fact that, if allowed to blaze down on them with untempered heat, even during the short time she is off the nest, it would be injurious to them; and therefore, on a hot morning, she does not leave them without first placing on the top of each a good pinch of sand. This she does in order that the germ—which, whatever side of the egg is uppermost, always rises to the highest point—may be shaded and protected. Having thus set her nest in order, she walks off, to fortify herself with a good meal for the duties of the day.

And now comes the white-necked crow's chance; for which, ever since at earliest dawn he drew out his artful old head from under his wing, he has been patiently waiting. An ostrich-egg is to him the daintiest of all delicacies; but, nature not having bestowed on him a bill strong enough to break its hard shell, he is only able, by means of an ingenious device, to regale on the interior. He carefully watches till the parent's back is turned, and she is a good distance from the nest; then, flying up into the air, he drops a stone from a great height with a most accurate aim, and breaks an egg. He makes good use of his quarter of an hour; and he, no less than the hen ostrich, has had an ample meal by the time the latter returns to the nest. Perhaps to-morrow she will not wander so far away.

This crow, inveterate egg-stealer though he is, has a most respectable and clerical appearance; and with his neat suit of black and his little white tie he looks indeed "unco guid." The Boers—possibly on account of this pious exterior—have a legend to the effect that these birds are the "ravens" which fed Elijah. They say that after the birds had carried the meat, a little of the fat remained on their necks; in commemoration of which their descendants have this one conspicuous white patch on their otherwise black plumage. Numbers of tortoise-shells, some of immense size, are found about the *veldt;* which have been broken in the same manner as the ostrich-eggs, and their inmates devoured, by these crows; who thus reverse the process by which, some twenty-three centuries ago, the eagle, dropping his tortoise on what seemed to him a convenient stone for his purpose, smashed the bald head of poor Æschylus.

Among the denizens of the *veldt* the crows, unfortunately, are not the only appreciators of ostrich-eggs:

and our worst enemies are the jackals. In lonely, far-off camps they plunder many promising nests; rolling the eggs away with their paws, sometimes to great distances. Occasionally, too, little chicks fall victims. We waged deadly war against the depredators; making liberal use of strychnine pills to "take us the foxes, the little foxes," which, finding no vines to spoil in the Karroo, were instead spoilers of ostrich nests. On a large vine-farm in the Atlas Mountains, where, after leaving the Cape, we spent some months, we were able to note the accuracy of this passage of Scripture—in which, I am told, the word rendered "foxes" ought in reality to have been translated "jackals." These animals did indeed work terrible havoc among the vines, eating incredible numbers of grapes; and T—— did much good by his introduction among them of the South African plan of poisoning, to which many succumbed. The pills, enclosed in pieces of fat, are dropped about the *veldt*; generally by a man on horseback, towing behind him a piece of very "high" meat, which, fastened by a *riem* (narrow strip of hide) to the horse's tail, drags along the ground. By-and-by the jackals, attracted by the odour of meat, come out; and, following along the route taken by the poisoner, find and eat the tempting pieces of fat. In the morning a good number are sure to be found dead; the survivors, apparently concluding that there is something very wrong about the place, take themselves off for a time to another neighbourhood; and the comparative silence which reigns at night is a pleasant change after the chorus of their querulous, uncanny voices.

The partiality of jackals and crows for ostrich-eggs, expensive though it is to us, reflects credit on their taste; for the eggs are certainly delicious. Those which, being useless for setting, found their way into my kitchen, were always most acceptable; and I have never had lighter cakes, nicer omelettes, custards, etc., than those made from them. And then they go so far! Two large square biscuit tins can be filled to overflowing with a noble batch of sponge finger biscuits, for which only one egg has been used. In spite of its large size — equalling twenty-four fowls' eggs — an ostrich-egg has no coarse flavour. It takes an hour to boil one hard; in which state it is a splendid article of food for baby ostriches.

Ostrich-eggs were much prized by the ancient Egyptians; and Gardiner Wilkinson tells us that they "were required for some ornamental or religious use, as with the modern Copts; and, with the plumes, formed part of the tribute imposed by the Egyptians on conquered countries."

Not long ago, T—— and I were much amused by the discovery, among copious notes in an old Bible dated 1770, of the following passage from a quaint old writer: "The Ostrich, which the *Arabians* call *Naama*, is a wild Bird of the Shape of a Goose, but much bigger than that; it is very high upon its Legs, and has a Neck of more than four or five Spans long: The Body is very gross, and in its Wings and Tail it has large Feathers black and white (like those of the Stork) and some grey; it cannot fly, but it runs very fast; in which it is much assisted by the Motion of its Wings and Tail: And when it runs, it wounds itself with the Spurs which it has on its Legs. It is bred in the dry Desarts, where there is no Water, and lays ten or twelve Eggs together in the Sand, some as large as a great Bowl, and some less. They say this Bird hath so little Memc᎑ʳ that as soon as she hath made an End of layin her Eggs, she forgets the Place where she left them so that when the Hen comes to a Place where ther are Eggs, let them be her own or not, she sets abrood upon them, and hatches them; and as soon as the Chickens are hatched, they immediately run about the Country to look for Meat; and they are so nimble, when they are little, before their Feathers grow, that 'tis impossible to overtake them."

One is inclined to think that the old author, Marmol, from whose "History of Africa" the above passage is quoted, cannot have written from any very accurate acquaintance with the Dark Continent; at any rate, it is not likely that he ever saw an ostrich, or he would have known that it possesses no spurs.

It is a strange fact that the most savage ostrich, if he comes up and finds you between himself and his nest, does not, as would naturally be supposed, rush to defend his eggs, and, if possible, kick you to death, but is instantly changed into the most abjectly submissive of creatures. "'Umble" as Uriah Heep, he squats at your feet; making a peculiar rattling noise with his wings, biting the ground, snapping his bill, closing his eyes, and looking the very embodiment of imbecility as he meekly implores you to spare his eggs. This suppliant posture is, however, not to be trusted; and, if tackey-less, you had better remain at the nest until assistance—or night—comes, for if once the positions of yourself and bird are reversed, "Richard's himself again." He squats, no longer in servile entreaty, but in defiance; and his challenge is promptly followed by a charge. The hen ostrich, being destitute of a voice, has but one way of calling her chicks, which is by that same rattling and rustling of the wings.

In strong contrast to the usual anxiety of the paternal ostrich for his nest was one case of which we heard. In a breeding-camp, containing a cock and two hens, troublesome complications had arisen. One hen persisted in sitting, while the other was as resolutely bent on laying; and, the struggles of the two rivals for the possession of the nest being extremely perilous to the eggs, the Boer to whom the trio belonged removed the laying hen from the enclosure. Now came the cock's turn to be excited. The departed hen was evidently his favourite wife; and, disconsolate at her loss, he ran restlessly about the camp for some time, *brooming* repeatedly; then, as if struck by some sudden impulse—probably of spite against his master —he ran to the nest, on which he deliberately jumped till he had broken every egg.

One of our birds was a morose old bachelor. Whether he had remained single from choice, or whether his surly temper had made him so unpopular that no hen would cast in her lot with him, we knew not; but there he was, living in solitary grandeur on the lower slope of our big mountain. Every time we took a certain favourite walk, a portion of which he had marked out as his beat, he would dispute the right of way with us; resenting the invasion of his solitude with more fuss than was ever made by the father of the largest family of chicks. Sometimes he would lie in ambush, and rush out at us from unexpected places, with all the artfulness of a rogue elephant. Fortunately, his domain being on the mountain-side, there was plenty of high bush, behind which it was not difficult to dodge him.

CHAPTER VII.

OSTRICHES (*continued*).

Vagaries of an incubator—Hatching the chicks—A bad egg—Human foster-mothers—Chicks difficult to rear—"Yellow-liver"—Cruel boys—Chicks herded by hen ostrich—Visit to Boer's house—A carriage full of ostriches—"The melancholy Jaques"—Ostriches at sea — A stampede — Runaway birds — Branding — Stupidity of ostriches—Accidents—Waltzing and fighting—Ostrich soup—An expensive quince—A feathered Tantalus—Strange things swallowed by ostriches—A court-martial—The ostrich, or the diamond?—A visit to the Zoo.

An incubator, considerably increasing as it does the number of chicks that can be hatched, is of course of the greatest value on a farm. We had one, capable of holding sixty eggs; and a "finisher," in which thirty more could be placed. Two paraffin lamps, kept constantly burning, heated the large tank of the incubator; and a thermometer, inserted in the water, had to be carefully watched in order that the temperature of the latter might neither exceed nor fall below 103°. Beneath the tank—so that the eggs, as in nature, might be heated from above—were four drawers, each with compartments for fifteen eggs. I was appointed manager of the incubator; and morning and evening—

following the example of the hen ostrich—I gave the eggs their quarter of an hour's cooling by allowing the drawers to stand open; also, as she does, I carefully turned each egg.

The regulation of the temperature was a matter of some anxiety, and enabled me—especially on first undertaking the work—to form a very good idea of the responsibilities of a vestal tending the sacred fire. Some mischievous imp seemed to be perpetually at work causing that thermometer to indulge in the wildest vagaries. Perhaps just one degree of the required temperature would be wanting; and though, for the best part of the morning, I had been coming anxiously every ten minutes or so to look at the thermometer, it refused, with all the perversity of "a watched pot," to rise above 102°. Then at last, a little off my guard, and absorbed in one of the numerous other home duties, I might possibly forget the incubator's existence for a little while; and, on suddenly remembering and running to it, find that the treacherous mercury had jumped up two or three degrees. Then the drawers would have to be thrown open, and the contents of several jugs of cold water wildly dashed in through the opening at the top of the incubator—and when at last, by still trembling hands, the thermometer was readjusted in the said opening, it would probably register as many degrees *below* as it had just been above 103°. T—— was away for three weeks during the time the incubator was in full work; and so great was the anxiety which haunted me, lest on his return I should present him with some sixty cooked birds, that I set an alarum every night for two o'clock, to assure myself that the temperature was playing me no tricks.

When within about eight or ten days of hatching, the chick can be felt moving about in the egg; and later on, when nearly ready to come out, he is heard squeaking, and tapping with his bill against the shell. Then at last, one day, when you come to turn the eggs in the finisher, where they are placed for the last fortnight, you find one with a hole in it—generally a three-cornered piece is knocked clean out—and in the opening a pinkish, soft-looking bill is making impatient movements, and a bright eye is peeping at you as knowingly as though already well acquainted with all the ways of a world on which its owner has yet to enter. An ostrich, by the way, seems far more intelligent as a baby than he ever is in after life.

A strong chick is generally able to free himself, by his own unaided efforts, from the shell; but if after a certain number of hours he is not out, it becomes necessary to assist him. This, however, requires extreme gentleness and caution, as there is great risk of inflicting injury; and, although I have helped many young ostriches into the world—losing but one patient in all my practice—I always preferred leaving that delicate work to nature. And yet there is something so tempting about these little half-opened parcels; one always longs to undo them and have a full view of the contents. The moment the little fellow is out of the egg, he seems to swell out, and looks so large that you wonder how he can possibly have been packed away in such a small space; and I am quite sure that the task of replacing him in the shell would as far surpass the powers of "all the king's horses and all the king's men," as did the reintegration of Humpty Dumpty.

Occasionally—and even at this time and distance it is hardly to be recalled without a shudder—the incubator would contain a bad egg. Imagine all the horrors of a bad hen's egg, multiplied by twenty-four! The whole drawer would be so pervaded by the odour that it was difficult for some time to discover the actual offender; and when at last it revealed itself by an uncanny moisture exuding through the shell, an amount of courage and caution was required for its removal and safe depositing outside, which suggested very flattering comparisons of one's own conduct with that of a soldier winning the V.C. by carrying away a live shell.

An incautious friend of T——'s was too closely investigating a doubtful ostrich-egg, when it exploded with a loud report. He was an old gentleman, with a beautiful white beard; and his condition, as described by T——, who—luckily from a safe distance—witnessed the accident, is best left to the imagination. Suffice it to say that an immediate and prolonged bath was imperative, and that a whole suit of clothes had to be destroyed.

In the days when chicks were so valuable, people who did not possess incubators sometimes had recourse to a strange way of hatching those eggs which, during the sitting, were either left orphaned by accident, or, as in the case of Jackie, deserted in consequence of floods. Some poor old Hottentot woman would be carefully tucked up, in company with the eggs, under numerous blankets,—where she would remain bedridden until she had hatched out the last chick. Sometimes, even, the stout, lethargic Dutch *vrouw* herself, to whose indolent nature the task was doubtless congenial enough, would perform the part of foster-mother.

When, either by natural or artificial means, the little ostriches are safely brought into the world, the farmer's next anxiety is to keep them there. They do well enough on the coast; but in the Karroo they are most difficult to rear, and our experience with them has been sad and disheartening. Numbers of them die, when about a month or five weeks old, from an epidemic which comes and goes in the strangest manner. During a whole season, for instance, one farmer will lose nearly every chick; while brood after brood will be successfully reared by another at no very great distance. Next year, perhaps, it is the turn of the latter to be the sufferer; and *vice versa*. Our unlucky year had a most promising beginning, unusually good rains having filled the country with nests; yet at the end of the season all we had to show of the rising generation of ostriches was a poor little troop of fifteen lanky, ragged-looking creatures, which through some rare toughness of constitution had survived the perils of infancy—over two hundred having succumbed.

The disappointment of losing the chicks is much intensified by the fact that they always begin so well. For the first three weeks nothing can be more encouraging than the appearance of the stout, sturdy toddlers; they eat voraciously and are full of life and spirits, waltzing, in absurd imitation of their elders, to show their joy on being first let out in the morning— the effort usually ending in a comical sprawl on the back.

Again and again comes the delusive hope that the spell is broken at last; that the luck has turned, and that *this* little brood is really going to live. But alas! —one morning, during that fatal fourth week, you notice that one little head, instead of being held up saucily and independently, is poking forward and downward in a dejected manner with which you are only too well acquainted. You know at once that the owner of that head is doomed, and that it will not be long before most, if not all, of his brethren show the same dreaded symptom. The disease is quite incurable —indeed, I have never known of an ostrich, old or young, recovering from any illness whatever; and though we tried all possible kinds of medicine, diet, and treatment, resolutely refusing to despair of any case while a spark of life remained, those chicks persisted in dying, sometimes at the rate of three or four a day. I was hospital nurse, and so deeply did I take to heart the loss of patient after patient that it became a joke with T——; and a plentiful sprinkling of grey happening just at this time to make its appearance on my head, he still attributes each silver thread to a little dead ostrich. A post-mortem examination of chicks which have died of this disease shows the liver to be of the bright colour of orange-peel.

Internal parasites also destroy a good many chicks; and altogether the little lives are precarious, and every troop of young birds successfully reared in the Karroo is a triumph.

For the first two or three months the chicks are herded near the house by boys, whose duty it is to keep them well supplied with prickly pear leaves and other green food, cut up small. This work ought to take up the greater part of the young herd's time; but—small boys being no more satisfactory as servants in the Karroo than they are anywhere else—we found it necessary to keep a very strict watch; and often during the day, however busy I might be, I would "make time" to run down to the shady spot which was the chicks' place of encampment—generally to find the infants hungry, and their useless nurse either asleep or plunged in some absorbing business of his own with a knife and a piece of wood. Sometimes, too, the boys, getting impatient with the chicks, were rough and cruel; one budding criminal especially was several times caught making footballs of his innocent charges, kicking them up several feet into the air. And on a farm where T—— was once staying, a juvenile black fiend was found to have deliberately broken the legs of some twenty chicks under his care; and, when asked the reason of his conduct, said, "They run about, give me too much trouble."

The chicks are often attacked by old birds—always spiteful to little ones which are not their own—and we have had several kicked to death by their vindictive elders. On a neighbouring farm, however, dwelt the usual exception to the rule, in the shape of an old hen, which—although herself not a mother—showed such a strong affection for chicks, and took such devoted care of them, that at last, much to her delight, she was appointed to the post of herd, *vice* the small boy, dismissed as incorrigible. She filled the place of the latter far better than he had ever done; leading the little creatures, with the greatest care, wherever the tenderest *veldt* was to be found; never losing her temper with them, or failing to bring the full number home to bed at sundown; and altogether acquitting herself in a wonderfully sedate and business-like manner for so scatter-brained a creature as an ostrich.

Her history ought of course to have ended here; but truth compels me to state that at last, after she had successfully brought up many families of chicks, and had come to be respected and trusted as the steadiest and most useful of farm-servants, one day the idiotic ostrich-nature asserted itself; she took a sudden and senseless fright—probably at nothing—lost her wits, bolted right away, leaving the chicks to get dispersed about the *veldt*, where only a few were found; and was herself never heard of again.

I think our friends at home would have been rather amused if they could have seen us one day, driving home from Mount Stewart with *twelve ostriches* in our extremely small American spider. On our way to a farm where T—— had business we happened to pass a Dutchman's house, round the door of which we noticed a lively little brood of chicks running about. T—— of course no sooner saw them than he coveted them (he frankly confesses himself quite unable to keep the tenth commandment as far as ostriches are concerned); and we pulled up, accepted the hospitable invitation of the Boer, who doubtless read in our eyes the chance of "doing a deal," and went into the house, where, first of all, a solemn, silent, and apparently endless course of hand-shaking had to be gone through. The Cape Dutch living in very patriarchal fashion, there were not only a wife and many sons and daughters, but a well-preserved parental couple, a mother-in-law, several sons and daughters-in-law, and—needless to say—a crowd of children of all sizes, including two babies. All but the two last came forward one after another and gravely took our hands; then we all sat round the room, solemnly looking at each other, and T—— and I felt as if we were at a funeral. We would have been thankful to have fled; but—our own birds not having begun laying—we did so want those chicks, and we felt that it was worth while to endure something for their sakes.

Presently coffee was handed round in huge cups, evidently more than half filled with sugar. The more highly the good *vrouw* wishes to honour you, the more horribly and sickeningly she over-sweetens your cup of tea or coffee; and the syrup we had to drink on this occasion left no doubt as to the kindly feeling of our hosts towards us. The entrance of the tray was the signal for conversation to commence; and, once set free, it flowed abundantly. As we sat drinking our coffee and talking of everything *but* the business on which we were bent, our thoughts flashed back to Oriental *bazaars*, where these identical preliminaries are necessary to every bargain. The relationship of everybody present to everybody else was accurately explained to us, with much pointing, or clapping on the back, as the case might be; and we in our turn were minutely questioned as to our names, ages, number of brothers and sisters and other relatives, etc.; the women again bringing back Eastern recollections by their resemblance to the inquisitive, chattering inmates of harems. Then T—— ventured to lead the conversation round to the coveted chicks; but it was a little too soon, the subject was abruptly dropped, and we again waded through all manner of irrelevant talk until, a becoming time having elapsed, and the requirements of etiquette being satisfied, the business was allowed to commence.

After such an inauguration, it may well be imagined that the bargain was not concluded in a hurry; and we had paid a tediously long visit before we were at last the happy possessors of the chicks for which we had suffered so much; and, putting them loose into the spider at our feet, where—being about as large as ducks—they made rather a tight fit, drove off with them.

A little further on, at another Dutchman's house,

and with more bargaining, we bought a young *paauw* (pronounced " pow "). This game bird (the great bustard) grows to an immense size, some being occasionally shot which measure nine feet across the outspread wings; but fortunately—considering the number of passengers already on board—the present specimen, being but a chick, was no larger than a fine fowl.

When we arrived at last at our original destination, the young ladies of the house presented us with a pretty little baby hare, which had just been caught; and with this wee creature nestling in my lap, and the *paauw* and the ostriches all scrambling about among our legs and apparently not on the best of terms, we drove the twenty miles home. The poor *paauw* was very unhappy, and kept bewailing his fate in a long, weird cry, like the moaning of the wind; whence he immediately acquired his name of "the melancholy Jaques." We had an amusing though rather anxious journey; for the spider—consisting simply of a kind of magnified Japanese tea-tray, supporting the lightest of seats, and mounted on four wheels, almost bicycle-like in their slenderness—was hardly the safest thing in which to convey restless live stock which was not fastened or secured in any way. The road, too, was terrible; indeed, in one place it resembled a steep, rocky staircase, and after every bad jolt I looked anxiously back to see if any of our creatures were lying on the ground. Thanks to T——'s careful driving, however, we brought the whole collection safely home, none the worse for their long journey.

Jaques, I may as well mention here, soon grew very tame; but, being—we never knew why—persistently snubbed by all the other pets, was driven to the companionship of the fowls, with which he struck up a close friendship; spending most of his time among them, and always coming with them to be fed. He would also forage about in the kitchen for scraps; and, if disappointed in his search, would utter his desponding cry, and seem quite heart-broken. He was a handsome bird; with delicately-pencilled plumage of different shades of grey and brown, a little neat crest on his head, and absurdly small feet, which looked as if they could not possibly support so large a body. Unfortunately, poor Jaques did not live to attain his full size, but poisoned himself with pumpkin seeds; which had been carelessly dropped on the kitchen floor, in spite of repeated orders that these seeds—being a deadly poison to turkeys—should always be instantly burnt as soon as a pumpkin was cut open. We lost several of our turkeys through the neglect of this rule by the stupid Hottentot girls.

Although little ostriches are such good travellers, it is anything but easy to transport full-grown ones about the world. They are wretched sailors, as T—— has found to his cost; for when, some time ago, he took several pairs of birds to Sydney, about half of them died at sea. The day before they were shipped from Port Elizabeth they were placed in a store where there was a large quantity of tobacco, on which some of them regaled, with the consequence that before they had been at sea a week three were dead from nicotine poisoning. T—— does not mind a story told against himself, so I may mention that a plan adopted by him with a view to ensuring the comfort and cleanliness of the birds during the voyage did not—as regards the former advantage—turn out quite a success. He carpeted the pens with cocoa-nut matting; and when the vessel began to roll, and the birds sat down, their legs were terribly chafed and rubbed by the roughness of the matting. And although T——, to procure rag wherewith to bind up their sores, recklessly sacrificed shirts, pocket-handkerchiefs, and whatever other linen came to hand, several succumbed. The survivors did so well in Australia that arrangements were made to carry on ostrich-farming in that country on a large scale; and T—— was about to export two hundred birds when the Cape Government, hearing of the project, imposed an export duty of £100 on every ostrich, and £5 on each egg.

Ostriches are very bad railway travellers; and avail themselves of every possible opportunity of coming to grief in the cattle-trucks; in which they often seem to be too closely packed. And as for their behaviour when travelling on foot, T—— has had some experience of the infinity of trouble they can give to those in charge of them. Having once bought a troop of ninety birds on the West Coast, he accompanied them himself on the long journey to Port Elizabeth. One night there was a stampede; and when daylight broke over the vast plain not one ostrich was in sight. Of course "there was mounting in hot haste;" and poor T—— had to ride about the country after the runaways, which were so dispersed that they could only be collected by twos and threes. He had two days of very hard work before he succeeded in getting them all together again.

When T—— first started ostrich-farming, a good many years ago, he and his partners—little knowing the "kittle cattle" with which they had to deal—thought they would do without fencing. They soon found all their birds gone; and had to scour the country for hundreds of miles in pursuit of their erratic stock, riding all their horses to death.

Profiting by this sad experience, T—— has carefully fenced Swaylands in all directions except where the steepness of the mountain forms a natural barrier. Yet in spite of all the trouble and money spent—and enclosing is one of the heaviest of all expenses incurred in starting a new farm—our birds were continually getting away. We have unfortunately the great disadvantage of a high-road running straight through the farm; and often a lazy Boer, thinking it too much trouble to kick away the stone with which he had propped the gate open while his waggons passed through—though T—— had carefully adjusted that gate to fall to and close itself—would cause the loss of several of our birds; which of course might or might not be heard of again. On one occasion over twenty birds seem to have gone out in a body, owing to the gate being left open; and only a few were eventually recovered.

Some birds—artful old rovers who have been away before and have tasted the joys of freedom—will spend days running up and down along the side of the fence; keeping the gate well in sight, and watching for the chance of its being left open.

The family of one of our herds, living close to a gate, were supposed to act as lodge-keepers; but—like most of the coloured race—they could never be induced to attend steadily and systematically to their duty, and we often found the gate wide open, inviting an exodus of birds. A fine of five shillings was imposed for each offence; but the hardened sinners knew that T——'s kind heart made him reluctant to enforce the penalty.

Ostriches, when very firmly bent on escaping, and finding no gate open, will sometimes charge the fence; and, though occasionally one will succeed in tumbling safely over and getting away, the clumsy performance most frequently results in broken legs.

Runaway birds are far from being the least among the many trials of an ostrich-farmer's life; and the annual losses caused by them even exceed in number those resulting from accident. Then they involve such endless waste of time and trouble. T—— was continually riding about, searching and making inquiries, often in vain, for lost ostriches. When he was fortunate enough to find one, or hear of its whereabouts; or perhaps see, from the advertised description of its brand, that it was an inmate of some distant pound, two of the herds—never spared without difficulty from other work—would be sent, often a long journey of three or more days, to bring it back.

A returning runaway, always a joyful sight to us, was also rather a laughable one. As he was marched along between the two men, each with a tight grip on his shoulder, he looked just like a pickpocket in the hands of the police, going to prison; and a large piece of sacking, roughly sewn round his body to give his captors a firmer hold, made him appear as though already in convict dress. Then, to prevent his giving trouble on the road, his head would be in a bag. As often as not this bag would be one of my pillow-cases, surreptitiously abstracted by T—— from the linen-drawer before sending off the men.

The very necessary operation of branding is performed on the ostrich's large, bare thigh, which seems just made for the purpose. Sometimes a considerable number of our young or newly-purchased birds would be branded at once. The irons with our brand, the Turkish crescent, were heated in a little portable forge placed in one corner of the plucking-kraal; and each poor bird in turn received the mark of our ownership with an agonized start on one side; the smell, and the hissing sound of the frizzling flesh always reminding me unpleasantly of the horrible performances of the Aïssaoua, which (because every one else went) I was once foolish enough to go and see in Algiers. Old birds, which have frequently changed hands, sometimes display a fine collection of initials and different designs, covering both thighs.

Unfortunately, branding is not always the safeguard against theft which it is intended to be; for there are quite as many dishonest people in the Cape Colony as elsewhere (if not rather more), and it is no uncommon trick to obliterate the brand of a bird which has come astray by applying over it a much larger one —a "frying-pan" brand, as one hears it occasionally called by victims.

As regards the stupidity of ostriches, although indeed they are falsely accused on one point; that of hiding their small heads in the sand and imagining therefore that their large bodies are quite invisible to the foe, they do many other things quite as foolish, and—to revert again to the Book of Job—their character could not possibly have been more perfectly summed up than it is in the words: "Because God hath deprived her of wisdom, neither hath He imparted to her understanding." And, indeed, no one looking at the ostrich's ridiculous little head, so flat immediately above the eyes as to leave no room for any brain, can wonder that he is an imbecile; possessing even less intelligence than a common fowl, and not recognizing the man who has fed him every day for years, if the latter comes to the camp in a coat or hat to which he is unaccustomed. A friend of T——'s was attacked and knocked down by one of his own ostriches, an old bird which had been constantly fed by him, but which, on seeing him for the first time in a black hat, took him for a stranger. Fortunately T—— was with him, and, having brought a tackey—in spite of assurances that none would be needed—came promptly to the rescue.

Ostriches are long-lived creatures; indeed, it is impossible to say what venerable age they may be capable of attaining, for, however old they become, they never show any signs of decrepitude, nor do their feathers deteriorate; while, as for an ostrich dying of old age, I do not believe any one has ever heard of such a thing. But it is accident which, sooner or later, ends the career of nearly every ostrich; and in about ninety-nine cases out of a hundred the disaster is, in one way or another, the result of the bird's own stupidity. There surely does not exist a creature—past earliest infancy—more utterly incapable of taking care of itself than an ostrich; yet he is full of conceit, and resents the idea of being looked after by his human friends; and when, in spite of all their precautions for his safety, he has succeeded in coming to grief, he quietly opposes every attempt to cure his injuries, and at once makes up his mind to die. If his hurt is not sufficiently severe to kill him, he will attain his object by moping and refusing to eat—anyhow, he dies—often apparently for no other reason than because his master, against whom he has always had a grudge, wishes him to live. He seems to die out of spite; just as a Hindoo servant will starve himself, waste rapidly away, and finally come and expire at the gate of the employer with whom he is offended.

The worst and most frequent accidents by which ostriches contrive to make away with themselves are broken legs; these—even were the patients tractable—it would be impossible to cure, owing to the strange fragility of that limb which, as we have seen, is capable of inflicting so deadly a kick,—and any poor bird which breaks a leg has to be instantly killed. The bone seems almost as brittle as porcelain; and a comparatively slight blow is enough to splinter it into just such jagged and pointed fragments as result from breaking the spout of a china teapot.

One very fruitful source of broken legs is the dervish-like habit ostriches have of waltzing when in particularly good spirits, and especially when first turned out of the kraal in the morning. They go sailing along so prettily in the bright sunshine; their beautiful wings, spread and erect, giving them at a little distance the appearance of white balloons; but they have a sad tendency to become giddy and tumble down, and, knowing the frailty of their legs, we do not look with unmixed pleasure on the graceful performance. Some birds, indeed, have the sense to save themselves by "reversing," which they do as cleverly as practised human dancers; but the accomplishment seems rare among them, and we calculate that waltzing costs us eight or ten per cent. per annum.

Then they often fight savagely; and the terrific "thud" of the blows they deal upon each other's bodies makes one tremble lest the next kick should fall on one of the brittle legs; as indeed frequently happens. One day (a long drought having brought our birds round the house), two splendid young cocks began fighting close to the windows. In an instant one of them was down; with his leg snapped across, and all but knocked off, by a frightful blow. T—— being from home, I had to go and inspect the poor bird's injuries—a sickening sight—and do him the only kindness possible, that of ordering his immediate execution. A couple of hours later, some of the flesh from one massive thigh was simmering in my stock-pot, sending forth a most delicious odour; while both legs, joints from which indeed to "cut and come again," dwarfed the proportions of the Angora meat as they hung beside it, high out of reach of dog or jackal, in our open-air larder. For when by some untoward accident, such as that just described, our birds came suddenly by their death, we had the very small and melancholy consolation of eating them. That is to say, following the example of French frog-eaters, we ate the legs only; there being no meat whatever on any other part of the creature's body. Instead of having a nice plump breast, like that of a fowl, turkey, or any other of the Carinatæ or keel-breasted birds, the ostrich has a flat breast-bone and large ribs shaped wonderfully like those of a human being. His body is always bony; and, however well you may feed him, the nourishment all seems to go to his legs. An unpleasant stringiness prevents ostrich-steaks from being quite nice, but the soup is perfection. I never tasted any quite equal to it; although some, made from the enormous tortoises found occasionally on the *veldt*, came very near it in goodness. The best beef-stock is not to be compared with ostrich-soup; and I imagine the latter would be a most nourishing food for invalids. An ostrich which has died in good condition has a large quantity of beautiful, soft, bright yellow fat. This, being most useful, is always carefully put away in jars; and there is no fat equal to it for guns, saddles, harness, boots, etc.

Besides waltzing and fighting, there are endless other ways in which ostriches—always ingenious in devising plans for their own destruction—manage to get their legs broken, and their throats consequently cut; but the favourite form of *felo-de-se* is collision with the wire fences. These seem to have some magnetic attraction for the *vogels*, as the Dutch call them—the word, appropriately enough, too, being pronounced "fools."

"Another bird killed in the wires!" How familiar any one living on an ostrich farm becomes with these words of woe! Anything, or nothing—the latter indeed more frequently—suffices either to frighten or embolden an ostrich into flinging himself headlong into the nearest fence. The appearance of a strange dog, for instance—and in spite of strict orders the Kaffirs always *will* bring dogs about the place—is quite certain, whatever may be the view taken of it by the ostrich, to lead but to one result. Say the dog is coming along on the opposite side of the fence. An imbecile boldness and pugnacity straightway inspire the ostrich; he has no eyes for anything but the dog, and, leaving the fence entirely out of his calculations, he makes a mad, blind charge, which lands him well in the wires; and if he is extricated from the latter with unbroken legs, his owner may be congratulated on a very unusual stroke of luck. If, on the other hand, the dog and bird

OSTRICH-CHICK.
(Photographed from case in Stanley and African Exhibition.)

OSTRICHES MEDITATING ESCAPE THROUGH DEFECTIVE FENCE.

are on the same side of the fence—then, even Burns's mouse had no greater "panic" in his "breastie" than that which impels the senseless biped to dash straight into the wires on his left; though miles of unfenced *veldt*, along which he might run with safety and soon distance the dog, stretch away to his right. The dog, of course, was not in either case troubling his head about the ostrich; and only wonders what all the commotion is about.

One of T——'s birds performed the "happy despatch" in quite a novel manner. Seeing a tempting quince growing on the further side of a hedge, he squeezed his head and neck through a narrow fork in the branches to reach it. Having secured and eaten his prize, he tried to draw his head back. But what was difficult enough before was now impossible; his neck, bulging with the quince, kept him a prisoner, there was no one at hand to help, and the more he tugged and jumped in the frenzied manner of ostriches when held by the head, the more firmly he stuck. And he was found at last, with his neck broken, and his head, to all intents and purposes, pulled off.

Another ostrich, running up against some projecting ends of wire, tore his throat open; inflicting so deep a gash as to divide the œsophagus. T—— (surgeon as well as everything else a colonist requires to be) went in quest of needle and thread to sew up the wound; and, on returning, found that his patient, having discovered a sack of mealies, was busily helping himself to the contents; though with the unsatisfactory result that the food, as soon as swallowed, tumbled out again through the slit in his throat. Nothing daunted, however, and apparently insensible to pain, the feathered Tantalus continued to feed; wondering no doubt why, having eaten so much, he remained hungry. Thanks to T——'s care, this bird, a rare exception to the general rule of wounded ostriches, actually recovered.

Talking of the ostrich's food-passage, it is rather a curious sight to watch the progress of a large bone, or of a good beakful of mealies, as it travels down the long throat of the bird. During its journey, the large, slowly-moving lump is seen to make the circuit of the whole neck, and while passing round the back of the latter it looks comical indeed. Queer things sometimes find their way down this tortuous passage; the excessive queerness of some of them giving rise to the frequent boast of those persons fortunately able to eat anything, fearless of consequences, that they "have the digestion of an ostrich." But those miscellaneous collections of old bones, glass and china, stones, jewellery, hardware, and odds and ends of all sorts, with which the creature stores his interior, till one is reminded of Mark Twain's "solid dog," fed on paving-stones—far from showing that an ostrich has a good digestion, are necessary to prevent his having a very bad one. They are, of course, simply his teeth, the millstones which grind his food; only they are situated in his stomach instead of in his mouth, and, on an immensely-magnified scale, they only perform the work of those grains of sand with which the little cage-bird keeps himself healthy. Certainly ostriches occasionally show a sad want of discrimination, and make choice of articles which are quite unsuitable for their purpose. The manager's lighted pipe, for instance, was snatched and greedily swallowed by one of our birds before any one could stop him; and for a while the thief was very anxiously watched to see if evil consequences would ensue. Luckily, however, the strange fare did not seem to disagree with him. Another bird picked a gimlet out of a post, in which, for one moment, it had been carelessly left sticking—tossed it down his throat, and was none the worse for it.

Ostriches, like magpies, are attracted by everything bright and glittering; hence the frequent and just complaints brought against them for theft. But their own interior is the only hiding-place where they bestow the precious stones and other articles of jewellery which, whenever they have a chance, they will always steal.

One day, while yet new to the colony, and to the ways of ostriches, I was standing with T—— by the side of one of the camps, looking over the fence at the birds, and much amused by the curious, dancing manner in which the creatures moved, as if hung on wires; when suddenly one of them, with a motion as quick as lightning, made a dash at my earring, a little round knob of gold, exactly the size and colour of a mealie (Indian corn seed), for which perhaps he took it; and I only drew back just in time to save it—and probably a piece of the ear with it—from going down his throat.

A newly-arrived gentleman was less fortunate. He,

too, was looking over a fence into a camp, when the sharp eye of an ostrich spied a beautiful diamond in his pin, and in an instant the jewel was picked out and swallowed. A kind of court-martial was held on the ostrich; the relative values of himself and of the diamond being accurately calculated, that his judges might decide whether he should live or die. Fortunately for him it was just the time when ostriches were expensive; and his value was estimated at £100, while the diamond was only worth £90. Those £10 saved his life; and the diamond was allowed to remain and perform the part of an extra-good millstone in his interior. Had he waited till the present time to furnish his internal economy thus expensively he would have been very promptly sacrificed. But people should not wear diamonds on ostrich farms.

When, soon after our return from the Cape, we were staying for a time in London, one of our first expeditions was to the Zoo. There, with great delight and amusement, we walked about, looking up one after another of our old South African friends. But it was a cold, gloomy day; and in the houses as well as out of doors the exiles from that sunny land seemed much depressed by their changed conditions of climate. The meerkats, curled up in a half-torpid state, were no longer the merry little rogues they had once been, when in happier days they stood on their hind legs outside their burrows, toasting their little backs in their native sunshine. The baboon was morose; the snakes sleepy; the African buffalo no longer terrible as in the wilds of his old home, but a poor dejected creature, utterly crushed and broken-hearted by long residence under cold, grey skies. Altogether, everything hailing from Austral Africa looked very homesick that dull day, with the sole exception of the secretary bird, which, after a long and persevering search—for old Jacob's sake—we at last succeeded in finding. He was a delightful bird; as tame as our own old friend, and evidently a great favourite with his keeper. We felt wickedly covetous, as the man, pleased at the interest we showed, put the intelligent bird through a number of comical performances, which included the "killing" of a stuffed ratskin, kept for the purpose of displaying how the secretary in his wild state beats to death the mice, lizards, and other creatures on which he feeds.

But where were the ostriches? Just as actors, when they have a holiday, usually spend it in going to the theatre, so, of all the creatures in the Zoo, those we were most anxious to see were the great birds of whose company during the last few years we might reasonably be supposed to have had enough. But no ostriches were to be seen; and the keeper of whom we inquired told us that all were dead. On asking the cause of death, we heard that it was "because the people fed them on pennies." We went to the office of the secretary of the gardens, and found that this statement was really true, and that the post-mortem examination of each poor bird had brought to light a large number of copper coins which had been swallowed. We were glad to hear that any ostriches kept in the gardens in future were to be separated by glass from a public idiotic enough to waste its money in poisoning them.

After this, we were quite able to believe a story told us of how a girl was one day seen at the Zoo, feeding these same unfortunate birds with some ten or twelve pairs of old kid gloves, evidently saved up for the purpose, and presented, one after another, tightly rolled up into a ball; the creatures gulping them down quite as a matter of course, and looking out for more.

CHAPTER VIII.

MEERKATS.

Meerkats plentiful in the Karroo—Their appearance—Intelligence—Fearlessness — Friendship for dogs — A meerkat in England—Meerkat an inveterate thief—An owl in Tangier—Taming full-grown meerkat—Tiny twins—A sad accident—Different characters of meerkats—The turkey-herd—Bob and the meerkat—"The Mouse."

THE little meerkats were surely created for the express purpose of being made into pet animals. Certainly no prettier or funnier little live toys could possibly be imagined. Nearly every homestead in the Karroo has its tame meerkat, or more likely two or three, all as much petted and indulged, and requiring as much looking after, as spoilt and mischievous children. In their wild state, these little creatures are gregarious, and live, like the prairie-dogs and biscachas of the Western Continent, in deep holes underground, feeding chiefly on succulent bulbs, which they scratch up with the long, curved, black claws on their fore-feet. They are devoted sun-worshippers; and in the early morning, before it is daylight, they emerge from their burrows, and wait in rows till their divinity appears, when they bask joyfully in his beams.

They are very numerous in the Karroo; and as you ride or drive along through the *veldt* you often come upon little colonies of them, sitting up sunning themselves, and looking, in their quaint and pretty favourite attitude, like tiny dogs begging. As you approach, they look at you fearlessly and impudently, allowing you to come quite close; then, when their confiding manner has tempted you to get down in the wild hope of catching one of them, suddenly all pop so swiftly into their little holes, that they seem to have disappeared by magic.

There are two kinds of meerkats; one red, with a bushy tail like that of a squirrel, the other grey, with a pointed tail, and it is this latter kind which makes so charming a pet. The quaint, old-fashioned little fellow is as neatly made as a small bird; his coat, of the softest fur, with markings not unlike those of a tabby cat, is always well kept and spotlessly clean; his tiny feet, ears, and nose are all most daintily and delicately finished off; and the broad circle of black bordering his large dark eyes serves, like the antimony of an Egyptian beauty, to enhance the size and brilliancy of the orbs. A curious kind of seam, starting from the middle of his chin and running underneath him the whole length of his body, gives him somewhat the appearance of a stuffed animal which has not been very carefully sewn up. His bright, pretty little face is capable of assuming the greatest variety of expressions, that which it most frequently wears when in repose being a contented,

A Meerkat.

self-satisfied smirk; impudence and independence displaying themselves at the same time in every line of his plump little figure. With his large, prominent forehead, giving evidence of the ample brain within, one need not, perhaps, wonder at his being one of the most sagacious of animals; although it is certainly almost startling to find all the intelligence of a dog in a wee thing which you can put in your pocket, or which, if buttoned up on a cold day inside the breast of your ulster, is as likely as not, when tired of that retreat, to squirm out down your sleeve. He is absolutely without fear; and with consummate coolness and audacity will walk up to the largest and most forbidding-looking dog, although a perfect stranger to him, and, carefully investigating the intruder on all sides with great curiosity, express disgust and defiance in a succession of little, short, sharp barks—" quark! quark! quark!" He is soon on the friendliest terms with all the resident dogs in the place; showing a marked preference for those possessing soft, long-haired coats, on which he evidently looks as a provision of nature existing solely for his benefit, and in which, like the little Sybarite that he is, he nestles luxuriously on cold days, chattering and scolding indignantly, with a vicious display of teeth, if the dog, getting up and going away, rudely disturbs his nap. Out of doors he is the inseparable satellite of the dog; and during strolls about the farm—in which, by-the-by, one is often attended by a motley crew of furred and feathered friends—the meerkat is sure to be seen following immediately in the wake of the dog, as closely as the latter follows master and mistress. Even a good long walk does not seem to tire his strong little legs, or, at any rate, if it does he is too plucky to give in and turn back, and as long as the dog keeps going on, he valiantly follows every *détour* of that animal's erratic course. Often, when starting for a ride or drive, we have been obliged to shut up our meerkat, so determined was he to come with us.

The astonishment of dogs in England at a meerkat brought home by us was most amusing. They would run after him, apparently taking him for some kind of rat; and when, to their amazement, instead of running away, he boldly trotted up to them, and, calmly and somewhat contemptuously surveying them, began to beg, they would hang their heads and draw back, with looks plainly expressive of their opinion that he was "no canny." It was fortunate for him that he inspired them with such awe, for otherwise he would certainly have died the death of a rat on one of the numerous occasions when he got away and wandered on his own account through the Kentish village where we were staying. The human natives whose cottages and shops he invaded, and to whom, with patronizing coolness and colonial absence of ceremony, he introduced himself, were scarcely less puzzled than the dogs at the queer animal we had brought from "foreign parts."

Every meerkat is an inveterate little thief; and if you leave him for one instant where a meal is prepared, you are sure on returning to see him jump guiltily off the table and make for the nearest hiding-place, chattering triumphantly as he goes, like a blackbird caught stealing fruit; an overturned milk-jug, dishes rifled of their contents, and sticky trails of butter, jam, or gravy across the tablecloth, proclaiming how profitably he has used his opportunity. He revels in mischief; and the reckless destructiveness in which he indulges, with no possibility of advantage to himself, but just for the fun of the thing, often brings you to the end of your patience. You vow that you will endure him no longer. You must get rid of him. The great Newton himself could not have pardoned such a constantly-offending Diamond. But the little rogue knows what is passing through your mind; and he knows, too, how to get on the right side of you. He assumes his prettiest attitude and his most benevolent smile; and as he sits bolt upright, turning his little head from side to side with quick, jerky movements, calling to you in the softest and sweetest of the numerous voices with which nature has endowed him, he is so irresistibly comical that, whatever he may have done, you cannot find it in your heart to be wroth with him very long. He is soon restored to favour; and then, to express his extreme contentment, he goes and lies flat on his stomach in the sunshine, with his legs stretched out straight. He is so flat that he seems all poured out over the ground, and looks like an empty skin. What becomes of his bones on these occasions is a constant source of wonder.

The only other creature I have seen capable of so

entirely changing its form at a moment's notice was a little owl we have since had in Tangier. This was a delightful pet, full of character and intelligence, though but a tiny thing not more than four inches high—a good part of this height consisting of the two long, ear-like tufts of feathers on the head. The absurd little fellow, who looked like one of the owl pepper-pots come to life, had many amusing ways; but what delighted us most about him was the startling abruptness with which not only his manner, but his whole appearance, even his shape, would change as if by magic, according to his frame of mind. He would sit, for instance, in a contemplative attitude, his eyes sleepily half-closed, his "ears" sticking up very straight, and his body looking extremely long and thin, as long as no one was interfering with him; but once disturb his repose, and instantly he would change his shape and become a fat little ball of soft fluffiness;—a grey powder-puff—with no ears visible, and two great yellow eyes glaring at you with the most ireful expression.

Unfortunately, relying too much on the tameness of our owl, and fearful of spoiling his beauty, we neglected the precaution of cutting one of his wings, in consequence of which we were one day left lamenting this prettiest of North African pets; and though we tried hard to procure another, explaining, with the little amount of Spanish at our command, to all the small boys in Tangier that we wanted "*un pajarito con orejas*" ("a little bird with ears,") we never looked upon his like again, and I imagine he must have been an uncommon bird.

The best chance of capturing full-grown meerkats is when, during long droughts, little companies of them are travelling in search of water; they often have to go long distances, and when they are thus far from their holes it is possible, though by no means easy, to run one down. In a few days, even if quite old when caught, a meerkat will know his name, come to you when called, or at least answer you with a little soft, bird-like note from whatever corner of the room he may be hiding in; scramble up into your lap, eat out of your hand, and altogether be nearly as tame as one which has been brought up in the house from infancy; though of course there is always the chance that, knowing the joys of liberty, he may some day, like the owl, take it into his head to desert.

T——, riding one day, and encountering a little travelling party of meerkats, gave chase on horseback. One of the animals, a very large, fat one, made for a hole, but found it a tight fit. He stuck fast, and T—— pulled him out ignominiously by the tail, and rode off with him. The mare—a wild, half-broken young thing—was so mad with fright at the way in which the little fury, though tethered by a handkerchief, dashed about, scratching and tearing at her sides, that she bolted all the way home. And when T—— set the new inmate down on the floor of the sitting-room, where it stood at bay, snarling savagely at us, it seemed about as unpromising a specimen on which to exercise our powers of taming animals as could well be imagined. But, refusing to be daunted, we began by tying our captive to the leg of the table, where he had to accustom himself to seeing us constantly passing and repassing; and though at first he tried to fly at us every time we came near, he soon saw that we had no evil designs against him, and was reassured by our careful avoidance of abrupt movements and sudden noises—most important of all rules to be observed in taming wild creatures. In a few hours he was sufficiently at home to drink milk—though cautiously and watchfully—from a teaspoon held out to him; and in four days he was following us about the house like a little dog.

This meerkat, the largest and handsomest we have ever seen, cannot have been anything less than the chief of his tribe. His powerful, tusk-like teeth, his unusually broad and capacious forehead, his superior intelligence, even for so clever a creature as a meerkat, all proclaimed him born to command. When one day he repaid the care and affection of many weeks by cruelly and ungratefully leaving us, we felt little doubt that, after giving civilization a fair trial, and comparing it with his old life, he had decided in favour of the latter, and started off home. We have often wondered whether he succeeded in finding his way back to his subterranean kingdom. And if so, did he find his subjects still faithful? or was he forgotten, and did another king reign in his stead?

One evening, when the men returned from the camps, one of the ostrich-herds displayed, nestling together in the palm of his hand, two baby meerkats, no larger than good fat mice, which he had caught in the veldt. Rewarding the captor, in the usual Karroo style of barter, with a pound of coffee, we took possession of his prize; and though at first our chance of rearing the tiny animals seemed doubtful, they flourished, grew up into fine specimens of their kind, and were among the most amusing of all our pets. They looked like a perfectly-matched pair of little images with heads moving by clockwork, as they stood, bolt upright, in their favourite places, one against each doorpost, and, critically surveying the view with an air of never having seen it before, revelled in the hot sunshine which came pouring in through the open doorway.

Unlike "birds in their little nests," and more after the unamiable fashion of human twins—who generally have to be sent to separate schools—they got on very badly together; and their frequent fights displayed most comically the strong contrast of the two energetic little characters. One of them was selfish and greedy, and, however liberal the supply of food presented— even though it were three times as much as he could possibly eat—always wanted all for himself. Jumping into the middle of the plate, he would stand—a miniature dog in the manger—noisily defending the contents against his gentler brother, whom he would attack and bite savagely if he ventured near. The other was a far nobler and finer character; and, though he too could "bark and bite" on occasion in an equally unbrotherly manner, it was no such base, material cause of jealousy which impelled him to do battle. Our notice and our affection were what *he* wanted all for himself; and so bitterly did he resent every kind word, every slightest caress bestowed on his companion, that it was the instant signal for war, and, flying at the other, he would attack him as vengefully as he in his turn was attacked at feeding-time.

Both brothers were on terms of insolent and contemptuous familiarity with Toto; on whom they looked as their slave, whom they made the butt for their jokes, and in the soft warmth of whose coat they slept as on the most luxurious of fur rugs. And when *he* wanted to sleep and *they* did not, how they relished the fun of keeping him awake against his will! What riotous games they would have, chasing each other backwards and forwards across his recumbent form, pulling his poor tired eyes open with their mischievous black claws, scratching and tickling his nose to make him sneeze, and trying their hardest to burrow into his ear or his mouth. One snap of his powerful jaws, and their frivolous career would promptly have been cut short; but the good old dog—who, in spite of all their teasing, loved the troublesome imps—submitted patiently, though they did make his eyes water.

One day, alas! tired out with play, they were comfortably nestling close up against their big friend's side, and all three were taking their afternoon nap. Perhaps Toto had a disturbing dream, perhaps the flies bothered him and made him restless,—at any rate during his sleep he rolled over on to one of the meerkats—our favourite, of course—and, all unconscious of what he was doing, crushed and suffocated the poor little fellow. Though no one thought of blaming Toto for what was purely accidental, he instantly and completely realized that he had caused the death; and as we stood lamenting over the flattened little body, the poor old dog's distress was most pathetic. He seemed quite overcome with shame; and as he stole from one of us to the other, timidly licking our hands, his expressive face pleaded eloquently for the forgiveness he had no need to ask. With all our efforts to reassure him it was a long time before his sensitive conscience recovered from the shock. The surviving little brother lived to a good old age, came home with us, and succumbed at last to the severities of an English winter.

The variety of character in our numerous meerkats formed quite an amusing study. They differed as much as human beings, and among them all there was but one which was stupid. He, poor fellow, met with injuries in early life at the hands of one of the cruel boys who looked after the little ostriches; who, in a passion with him for getting in the way, picked him up and flung him across the kitchen. He landed in a saucepan, received spinal damage, and grew up stunted in mind and body. And when, one day, he came suddenly to his end by tumbling into that disappointing fountain-basin of which mention has been made, we felt that on the whole it was rather a happy release.

One of our meerkats was the devoted ally of the turkeys, and would go out into the *veldt* with them every day; accompanying them on all their wanderings, and apparently looking upon himself as their herd. He would come trotting home with them in the evening, full of his own importance, and evidently taking to himself the credit of having brought them all safely back.

Another was fond of rambling off all by himself, sometimes going a very long way from home. On one occasion some friends from a distant farm, driving to call on us, saw near the road what they took for a wild meerkat, and set their collie at it. But animals have a wonderful instinct for detecting the difference between tame and wild creatures; and good Bob, dearly though he loved a scamper after any of the swift-footed denizens of the *veldt*, saw at once that this was not lawful game. So, instead of the expected chase, there was a friendly and demonstrative greeting between the two animals. The dog stood wagging his tail at the meerkat, the meerkat sat up " quarking " at the dog, and our friends, guessing that the little creature belonged to us, took him up into their Cape cart, and brought him to his home.

Another meerkat, being so incorrigibly savage that handling him was always attended with serious damage to the fingers, had to wear a muzzle, improvised for him by T—— out of one of the little wire baskets made for the spouts of teapots.

Another, though young and tiny, was a born tyrant; displaying the most overbearing and imperious of characters. In company with two full-grown meerkats, we brought him to England; the trio being taken on board the steamer in a large birdcage. There, however, owing to the truculent conduct of "the Mouse," as we called the little one, it was soon found impossible for all three to remain together; and separate quarters had to be provided for the two older animals. For the impudent mite, hardly out of babyhood, domineered over his seniors in most lordly fashion; forbidding them to take their share of the food, and dancing and jumping excitedly in the dish if they ventured to approach it; while they, although they could easily have made short work of the Mouse, calmly submitted; enduring his tyranny with that wonderful patience and forbearance so often shown by animals to one another under provocation which we human beings would bitterly resent. Perhaps they were overawed by the antics of the pugnacious atom, and thought he was not quite canny; or perhaps they looked leniently on his conduct as on that of a spoilt child accustomed to be humoured.

CHAPTER IX.

BOBBY.

Bobby's babyhood—Insatiable appetite—Variety of noises made by Bobby—His tameness—Narrow escape from drowning—A warlike head-gear—Bobby the worse for drink—His love of mischief—He disarms his master—Meerkat persecuted by Bobby—Bobby takes to dishonest ways—He becomes a prisoner—His clever tricks—Death of Bobby.

"Out of question thou wert born in a merry hour."

BOBBY was our tame crow. We brought him up from earliest infancy; indeed our acquaintance with him commenced when he was nothing but a speckled, reddish-brown egg, in a nest—or, rather, a flat, untidy bundle of sticks—in one of the few and stunted trees on the Klipplaat road. We were anxious to have one of these crows; knowing what intelligent and amusing birds they are, and having struck up a friendship with one on a neighbouring farm, a comical old one-legged fellow, with an inexhaustible fund of high spirits and solemn impudence, which made him a general favourite.

So we kept an eye on this egg; riding up to the tree occasionally, and watching the progress of the young bird through various stages of ugliness and bareness; until at last we took Bobby home with us, an ungainly, half-fledged creature, very unsteady on his legs and ragged as to his clothing, which latter indeed consisted more of stiff black quills than anything else. His immense bill was perpetually open; displaying the depths of his wide red throat as he shouted defiantly for porridge, of which he never seemed to have enough. He would take it with a loud, greedy noise, swallowing as much of your finger with it as possible, and apparently very much disappointed at having to let the latter go again. He seemed to live in hope that, if he only held on long enough, it would surely come off at last and slip quite down his throat. If we passed anywhere near his basket—even though he had just had an ample feed—he would shoot up, like a black Jack-in-the-box with a large red mouth, demanding more porridge. The vegetarian diet suited him, and he grew into a very large, handsome bird, with the glossiest and softest of blue-black plumage.

He soon refused to stop in his basket; tumbling out head first, and hobbling about the room; then, as his strength increased, he walked and flew about outside the house; always coming at night to sleep on our window. In the morning, as soon as it was light, he would fly in, and wake us up by settling on us and pecking us gently. Then, having given us his morning greeting, he would depart on his rounds outside; and presently we would hear him on the top of the house, or on the wire fence, practising some of his endless variety of noises; imitating the fowls, the donkeys, the dogs, or holding long conversations with himself, the greater part of which sounded like very bad language. One day we heard the cackling of a hen, which had apparently laid an egg on the top of the American windmill; and, on looking up, found that Bobby had selected this airy height as his practising-ground. It was one of his favourite places; and often, when there, he would catch sight of us the moment we came out of the house, and would come flying straight down to us, settling, sometimes quite unexpectedly, on a head or shoulder. He knew his name, and would come to us when we called him; unless indeed we had detected him in some mischief, when he would walk off, and keep carefully out of reach until he thought his offence was forgotten.

He was our constant companion out of doors; and when I went round to the store, gave out the men's rations, fed the ostriches and fowls, or superintended the washing, he was sure to be either following close at my heels like a dog, or perched on my shoulder, whispering confidentially in my ear in a most affectionate manner, while his bright little jewel of an eye watched all I did with great interest. His devotion to his master often led him to fly down the well after him, when work had to be done or superintended there. On one occasion he overshot the mark and got into the water, where he very narrowly escaped being drowned. He was pulled out with some difficulty, very wet and miserable, too frightened to know friends from foes, and biting his rescuer with all his might.

He would accompany us on our walks; and often took

long rides with T——, whose white sun-helmet became a most imposing headgear, as Bobby surmounted it, spreading his great black wings; reminding us of the raven-crest of some ancient Scandinavian warrior. Then, while in full gallop, he would dart after one of the great gaudy locusts—four inches long, and looking like painted toys daubed with red, yellow, and green—and, catching it on the wing with unerring aim, would fly back with it to his place on the sun-helmet, where he would regale with many noises expressive of satisfaction.

Bobby was not a "temperance" bird; indeed, his tastes lay in quite an opposite direction. We first discovered his propensity by accident, and in this manner. One day, when doctoring a sick fowl, which needed "picking up," I had mixed some porridge with wine, making it very strong. Just as I was about to administer it, Bobby came hurrying up, with his inquiring mind, as usual, all on the *qui vive* to see what was going on. He plunged his bill into the porridge, and helped himself to a large mouthful; then, finding it to his taste, he went on eating noisily and greedily, till he had "taken on board" a considerable amount, and walked off satisfied. Then, having attended to my patient, I went indoors, thinking no more of Bobby till, some time after, Nancy, our Hottentot "help," came running to us, calling out, "Missis! Missis! Bobby drunk!" We went outside; and there, sure enough, was Bobby, on his back, his little black feet helplessly kicking the air, his bill wide open, and a

M

variety of the most astonishing sounds proceeding therefrom, compared with which his usual, every-day profanity was mild.

He soon recovered, and was on his legs again, none the worse for the adventure; but it left him with a decided taste for stimulants, which he strove to indulge on all possible occasions. From that day he followed me to the store more pertinaciously than ever; sitting on the tap of the cask while I drew the wine for meals, bending down and twisting his neck to reach the stream as it flowed into the jug. He gradually learned to turn the tap himself, and was delighted if he could catch a few drops. At last he became clever enough to set the wine running altogether; and, as he never learned to turn the tap back again, great caution was necessary to see that he did not remain behind in the store, which he was always trying to do. He would often give a good deal of trouble by flying to the very topmost shelf, from whence it was difficult to dislodge him; and where a chase after him involved climbing over numerous sacks on my part, and much knocking over of bottles and tins on that of Bobby.

Bobby loved mischief; he revelled in it, not for the sake of any good which it brought him, but simply out of what the Americans call "cussedness." He was never so happy as when busily engaged in some work of destruction. When discovered, he would retreat to a safe distance, and, if pursued, would always manage to keep just out of reach; though not too far for you to see the twinkle of enjoyment in his wicked old eye, and hear his defiant croak; and as he strutted before you, looking back triumphantly over his shoulder, you felt that he was laughing at you.

The garden was his favourite field of operations; and, considering the time and trouble spent in producing that little oasis, and in persuading plants to grow in it, it was no small trial to be disappointed of one crop of vegetables after another, simply owing to his careful destruction of the young plants almost as soon as they showed their heads above ground. It was provoking, on going down to the garden, to find that the few rows of peas or French beans, which we had so carefully sown and watered, and which only the day before were coming up so promisingly, had been butchered to make Bobby's holiday, and were now all rooted up, dried and shrivelled in the hot sun, and lying, neatly arranged in order, each one in the place where it had grown. The culprit himself would probably be out of sight, for his gardening operations were usually carried on in the early morning, thus securing a quiet uninterrupted time among the plants before we were about; but once we caught him. We were out earlier than usual, and found Bobby so deeply engrossed in putting the finishing touches to a row of beans which he had pulled up and laid in their places with even more than his usual neatness, that he only looked up in time to see his offended master a few yards off, and just preparing to throw a good-sized stone. In an instant Bobby's mind was made up. Instead of attempting flight, and getting hit by the stone, he impulsively threw himself on T——'s generosity, and flew straight to his hand; looking up confidingly in his face, and at once winning the pardon he sought. His loving ways made us forgive many of his iniquities.

He liked to be "around" during meals; experimenting on the different articles of food, and occasionally dipping his bill into a cup of tea, or what pleased him still more, a glass of wine. But, unfortunately, he did not confine his attentions to the provisions, and was constantly attempting to carry off the spoons and forks: we narrowly escaped losing several of them, and he succeeded in getting away with one knife, which we never saw again. He also flew off with one of T——'s razors, and, when just above the middle of the dam, dropped it into the water.

At last his thieving propensities obliged us to forbid him the house, and Toto learned to chase him out the instant he appeared inside the door; the noisy hunt often ending in Bobby's being caught, and gently but firmly held down under the paws of Toto, who would lie wagging his tail contentedly, while Bobby, hurt nowhere but in his pride, vented his rage in discordant croaks. He became very jealous of Toto and the other pets which, less mischievous than himself, were allowed indoors; and he delighted especially in teasing the little meerkat, no less constant an attendant than himself among the small train of animal friends which followed us outside. Bobby would come up noiselessly behind, and, catching the tip of the meerkat's tail in his bill, would lift the little fellow off his legs, take him up a few feet into the air, and drop him suddenly. Then, after waiting a few moments till his victim had recovered his composure, and was off his guard, he would repeat the performance. The meerkat, a plucky, independent little character, resented the insult, and scolded and chattered vehemently, showing all his small teeth as he hung helplessly by the tail: but he was powerless against Bobby, and had to submit to being whisked up unexpectedly as often as his tormentor, by right of superior strength, chose to indulge his practical joke.

As Bobby grew older he lost his simple vegetarian tastes, despised porridge, and began to pick up a dishonest living about the fowl-house. He would fly to meet us in the morning, and perch on our shoulders with an impudent assumption of innocence; quite unconscious that the yellow stickiness of his bill told us he had just been breakfasting off several eggs. Then he took to eating the little chickens; and here his talent for mimicking the fowls stood him in good stead, and no doubt gained him many a dinner; his exact imitation of the hen's call to her young ones attracting victims within his reach. Many battles were fought by the maternal hens in defence of their progeny; in which Bobby always got the best of it, going off triumphantly with his prize, to regale in safety on the roof, or at the top of the windmill. Our poor little broods of chickens, which had enemies enough before in the shape of hawks, wild cats, snakes, etc., diminished rapidly with this traitor in the camp, whose capacious appetite was equal to consuming as many as four a day, with eggs *ad libitum*.

For this, and for his offences in the garden, Bobby was at last sentenced to be tied up: a little bangle of twisted wire was fastened round one leg, and attached to a long piece of stout wire outside our window; and there, so long as there were little chickens about the house, or tender young vegetables in the garden, he had to remain. We felt much compunction at treating our old friend thus, and feared that with his keen appreciation of freedom, and love of independence, he would pine in captivity; but Bobby did nothing of the kind. He was a far greater philosopher than we thought, and resigned himself at once to circumstances; making the best of things in a manner which some of the human race might well imitate. He harboured no resentment against us for depriving him of freedom; but, with his sweet temper quite unimpaired by his reverse of fortune, would give us just as warm and joyful a welcome, and caress us as lovingly, as in brighter days. He did not sit idle on the perch to which we had condemned him; but, his love of mischief breaking out in quite a new direction, he immediately consoled himself by commencing destructive operations on the window in which he sat, and on as much of the outside of the house as came within reach of his tether. He broke away the plaster from the wall, knocked out the mortar from between the bricks, and carefully picked all the putty out of the window, the panes of which he loosened so that they were always threatening to fall out; and in a very short time our room, which was in reality the newest part of the house, looked like an old ruin, with crumbling wall and dilapidated window.

He had a variety of resources at his command; and when not engaged in the destruction of the house, he would often be found busy on another work he had in hand, that of trying to free himself from his bonds. No human prisoner, filing through the iron bars of his dungeon, ever worked more perseveringly for his freedom than did Bobby,—biting through strand after strand of his cord of steel wires, or slowly, but surely, unfastening the twisted bangle on his leg; until at last some day he would be missing from his place—devastation in the garden, empty eggshells in the hens' nests, and sad gaps among the rising generation of fowls showing the good use he had made of his opportunities. No small amount of stratagem was required to recapture him when loose; and much time and trouble had to be expended, and tempting dainties displayed, to entice him within reach—a fat mouse, if there happened to be one in the trap, being the most effective bait.

Bobby would have been invaluable to an exhibitor of performing animals; his intelligence in learning the few tricks we had the leisure to teach him showed that he would have been capable of distinguishing himself if he had been educated as a member of a "happy family." We often brought him in to show his tricks before visitors; and his solemn way of performing them added much to the amusement he caused. He was a true humourist, and knew that his joke was more telling when made with serious face and grave deportment.

He would lie "dead," flat on his back, with his blue eyelids drawn up over his eyes; remaining motionless for any length of time we chose, and waiting for the word of command, when he would scramble to his feet in a great hurry, with a self-satisfied croak at his own cleverness. He would hang by his bill from one of our fingers, which he had swallowed to its point of junction with the hand; and, with his wings drooping, and his legs hanging straight down in a limp and helpless manner, looking altogether a most strange and grotesque object, would allow us to carry him about wherever we liked. A little string of dark red beads, brought from Jerusalem, would always throw him into a perfect frenzy of real or pretended fright—probably the latter; and if they were put anywhere near him, or, worse still, flung across his back, he at once commenced a series of startling antics, jumping and hopping about as if possessed, and uttering very uncanny sounds.

As the time for our return to England drew near, we made up our minds that we could not leave Bobby behind—he must be one of the little party of friendly animals which were to accompany us home; and we were already discussing in what kind of cage or box he should travel, wondering how he would like being enclosed in so small a space, and how he would behave at sea; friends in England had promised him a welcome, and were looking forward to seeing him—when, after all, we had to part with him. Just three weeks before we sailed poor old Bobby was suddenly paralyzed, and died in a few hours. We never knew what caused his death: whether his unconquerable curiosity had led him to eat something poisonous; whether the enforced sedentary life he had led for so many weeks together had undermined his constitution; or whether occasional dead snakes, and the contents of the mouse-traps, which during his detention were always contributed in hope of partially satisfying his large appetite, were perhaps unwholesome diet, and shortened his days, we cannot tell. But Bobby was sadly missed; and we still regret that brightest and most comical of all our pets.

Some will perhaps say, " What foolish people these must have been, to tolerate a black imp of mischief who destroyed their vegetables, ate their eggs, killed their chickens, did his best to pull down their house, and whose neck ought to have been wrung!" But, just as among the human race those characters we love best are not always the most faultless, so poor Bobby, full of imperfections as he was—far from honest, not always sober, and with that terrible bent for mischief making him so often a nuisance—yet possessed so many lovable qualities that his failings were redeemed; and he lives in our recollection as one of the kindest and most faithful of all our South African friends. We could have better spared a better bird.

CHAPTER X.

OUR SERVANTS.

A retrospective vision—Phillis in her domain—Her destructiveness—Her ideas on personal adornment—The woes of a mistress—Eye-service—Abrupt departure of Phillis—Left in the lurch—Nancy and her successors—Cure of sham sickness—The thief's dose—Our ostrich-herd—A bride purchased with cows—English and natives at the Cape—Character of Zulus and Kaffirs.

> " Man's work is from sun to sun,
> But woman's work is never done."

IT is always amusing, for those who have tried house-keeping in South Africa, to hear people in England talk of their "bad" servants. Ladies—who, after the short quarter of an hour devoted to interviewing the cook and giving the day's orders, need trouble themselves no more throughout the twenty-four hours as to the carrying out of those orders, but are free to pursue their own occupations, uninterrupted by a constant need of superintending those of their domestics,—sit in their beautifully-kept drawing-rooms or at their well-appointed dining-tables,—whose spotless linen and bright glass and silver are so delicious a novelty to eyes long accustomed to the Karroo's rough-and-ready back-woods style,—and, much to your surprise, complain bitterly of the unsatisfactory parlour-maid, or are pathetic over the iniquities of the cook who has just sent up a faultless little dinner. When any one, thus blissfully unconscious of what a really bad servant is, appeals to the lady colonist for sympathy, the unfeeling reply of the latter not unfrequently is: "You should try South African servants!" And instantly, before the mind's eye of that lady colonist, there arises a retrospective vision of the average "coloured help" of Cape farms; that yellow Hottentot or dark-skinned Kaffir, attired in a scanty and ragged cotton dress; her woolly head surmounted by a battered and not always over-clean *kappje* (sun-bonnet), or tied up in a red and yellow handkerchief of the loudest pattern, twisted into an ugly little tight turban. She stands, in the bright morning sunshine, against a background of dirty dishes and uncleaned saucepans, left neglected since last evening's meal; and of the comfort and advantage to herself of cleaning which before the adhering remnants of contents have dried and hardened it is absolutely impossible to convince her. Dogs, fowls, turkeys, and little pigs, in company with all the pet animals of the family and an occasional young ostrich, are kindly acting the part of scavengers on her unswept kitchen floor; where they are *habitués*, her wastefulness and untidiness affording them so good a living that they have grown bold, and, refusing to get out of your way, get under your feet and trip you up at every turn if you are rash enough to enter the dirty domain of their protectress. The latter, like some malevolent goddess, is surrounded by an atmosphere of most evil-smelling fumes, prominent among which is the paraffin with which, to save herself trouble, she liberally feeds the fire every time it becomes low; while the dense smoke and steam arising from several pots and saucepans on the stove proclaim the contents to be in various stages of burning,—the climax being reached by what was once the soup, but of which nothing now remains but a few dried and charred fragments of bone, tightly adhering to an utterly ruined pot—new last week. In answer to all expostulation the doer of the mischief has no word of regret or apology, but, taking the occurrence as a matter of course, shows all her even white teeth in a bright, good-tempered smile, as she says, "Yes, missis, de soup is burnt."

Then still more horrible whiffs assail you, viz., the combined odours of the various articles of food which she has put away, carefully covered up in jars and tins, where she has forgotten them; and where, in the close atmosphere of her stuffy kitchen, with the thermometer at 100°, they have promptly gone bad. She has no "nose"; and, though her kitchen may be pervaded with odours which knock you down, she remains smiling and contented, and needs to be informed of the fact that there is a bad smell before she will set to work—with great surprise—to hunt out the cause of it; too often revealing sights which make you shudder.

If it is anywhere near a meal-time, her fire is sure to be very low, if not out altogether; she has, of course, forgotten to tell the men, before starting for the camps in the morning, to chop wood for her day's needs; and as they, like all the coloured race, never perform the most every-day duty unless specially reminded, she has to do this work herself, with much difficulty and dawdling; the luncheon or dinner being accordingly delayed indefinitely. If, on the contrary, it is between meals, and no cooking will be required for several hours, there is a roaring fire, over the hottest part of which the chances are ten to one that you will find the empty kettle; while you are fortunate indeed if in your immediate and anxious investigation of the boiler you are yet in time to avert irretrievable damage.

Any dirty water or refuse which is thrown away at all is flung just outside the kitchen door, where it lies in unsightly heaps and pools, attracting myriads of flies; a plentiful sprinkling of which, needless to state, find their way, in a drowned, boiled, baked, roast or fried condition, into every article of food sent to table. Occasionally a teaspoon is tossed out among the rubbish, and lies glittering in the sunshine, ready to tempt the first ostrich that happens to prowl past the door. A very frequent counting of plate is necessary; and indeed, with such careless and not always honest servants, it is best to have no silver in daily use.

Breakages are ruinously numerous; each rough-handed Phillis in succession having her own private hiding-place, generally in the middle of some large bush, where—in spite of the standing promise that any accident honestly confessed will receive instant pardon—the fragments of all the glass, earthenware, and china destroyed through her carelessness are quietly put away out of sight, and, as she hopes, out of mind. Then perhaps, one day, having a little time to spare, you are looking about among the bushes to find out where the white turkey lays, and suddenly see, gleaming out through the dark foliage, what you at first take for a goodly number of the expected eggs. But alas! on closer investigation you recognize the familiar patterns of your pretty breakfast and dinner services; chosen carefully in England, with bright anticipations of the colonial home for which they were destined. For a long time their number has been mysteriously but steadily decreasing; till now there are but two soup-plates left, the cracked and chipped vegetable-dishes cannot among them boast of one handle, and the tureen, being without a lid, has to be covered ignominiously with a plate. Egg-cups there are none, and their places have long been supplied—not altogether unsuccessfully—by napkin-rings.

Constant relays of cups and saucers, as well as of glasses, are needed from Port Elizabeth; a dozen of either lasting but a very short time in the coloured girl's destructive hands. Opportunities of getting things sent up to the farm do not present themselves every week; and to be provided, at one and the same time, with a sufficient supply of both glass and china is as unheard-of a state of affluence as was the possession, by poor Mr. Wilfer, of a hat and a complete suit of clothes all new together. An influx of unexpected visitors is sure to arrive at the time of greatest deficiency; and the wine at dinner often has to be poured into a motley collection of drinking-vessels, among which breakfast and tea-cups, in a sadly saucerless and handleless condition, largely predominate over glasses. Another time it is the china which is conspicuous by its absence; a large party of strangers who have outspanned at the dam are asked in to rest for an hour or two on their journey, and the hostess finds herself obliged to hand the afternoon tea to her guests in tumblers.

The linen fares no better at the hands of Phillis than does the china. The best table-cloths and most delicate articles of clothing are invariably hung to dry, either on ungalvanized wires which streak them with ironmould, or on the thorniest bushes available, from whose cruel hooks, pointing in all directions, it is impossible to free them without many a rent. You spend much time and trouble over the work of extricating them, remonstrate with Phillis for the hundredth time on her rough treatment of them, and soon after, passing again, find that, all having been spread out on the stony ground near the dam, right in the path of the ostriches coming up from the water, numerous muddy impressions of large, two-toed feet crossing and recrossing the linen necessitate the whole wash being done over again. Although a clothes-line and pegs are provided, they are contemptuously ignored, and—the latter especially—never used except under the closest supervision; thus handkerchiefs, socks, and all the lighter articles of wearing-apparel are allowed to go flying away across the veldt; where, on long rides, you occasionally recognize fragments of them flapping about dismally on the bushes.

A strict watch has to be kept on the table-napkins, or they are sure to be carried to the kitchen and pressed into the dirtiest of service as dish-cloths, lamp-cleaners, etc. However many kitchen-cloths and dusters may have been given out, you never find one which is fit to touch; nor, until experience has taught you to keep the paraffin and its attendant rags under lock and key, and yourself to superintend the cleaning and filling of the lamps, is there one cloth which does not communicate the smell and flavour of the oil to every plate, cup, and glass brought to table. Every cloth is saturated with grease, all have large holes burnt in them, and a good many have been deliberately torn into quarters, or into whatever smaller sizes Phillis may have judged convenient for her ends. She has spared only those which, with their broad pink-and-white borders—with "Teacloth" in large letters, and a little teapot in each corner—have pleased her eye, and struck her as suitable adornments for her person; and which accordingly you often find twisted round the woolly head in place of the red and yellow turban, or gracefully draped on neck and shoulders as a *fichu*.

Like other daughters of Eve, she possesses her due amount of vanity, and has her own ideas—though they are sometimes strange ones—on the subject of improving her personal appearance. If she is of a careful turn of mind, and mends her own dresses—though most frequently she wears them torn and buttonless, fastened together only by the numerous black or white safety-pins which she has abstracted—she scorns to patch with the same colour, or anything near it, but introduces as much variety as possible into the garment by choosing the strongest contrasts of hue and greatest diversity of materials. Thus her pink or yellow cotton dress will be patched with a piece of scarlet flannel or bright blue woollen stuff; the blue skirt, of which the latter is a portion, having been tastefully repaired with a large square of Turkey red.

One day a bottle of salad oil is dropped and broken on the sitting-room floor; and Phillis is called in to remove the traces of the accident. Why does she look so delighted as she goes down on her knees beside the unctuous pool? and why does she not proceed to wipe it up? The reason is soon seen when she prepares for action by whisking off her bright handkerchief-turban. Then the pallid palms of her monkey-like hands are plunged blissfully into the oily mess, and again and again vigorously rubbed over head and countenance, till the thick mass of wool is saturated and dripping like a wet sponge, and the laughing face shines like a mirror. She is far too much absorbed to notice the amusement her performance is giving to hosts and guests; and when all the late contents of the bottle have been successfully transferred to her person, she goes back in high glee to her kitchen, rejoicing in her increased loveliness.

The house work is no less of a failure than are the

kitchen and laundry departments. The art of bed-making has to be taught, with much patience and perseverance, to each successive untutored savage; who—if she has not come straight from some bee-hive-shaped hut where beds are totally unknown—has lived in a Boer's house where, when it is thought worth while to make the beds at all (by no means an every-day business) it is never done till the evening, when it is just time to return to them—and then is not done in a manner which at all accords with English ideas. In the morning, each portion of the room and each article of furniture which requires cleaning or dusting must be separately and individually pointed out to your handmaiden; the corner where you do not specially tell her to sweep, and the table or bookshelf which you forget to commend to the attentions of her feather-brush, being invariably left untouched. It is the same with all the rest of her work; you have long ago found it impossible to make her understand a thing once for all, or to establish any sort of regular routine. She needs to be daily reminded of each daily duty, or it is not done. And then, unless under constant supervision, most wearying to her mistress, it is sure to be done wrong. Of course she never thinks of reminding *you* of anything, but is only too delighted if you have forgotten it. If, through some unlucky oversight, you have not told her to put the joint into the oven and the potatoes on the fire, the chances are that both will be found uncooked when the dinner-hour arrives. And even when all is ready to be served up, you must again remind her of each dish, and of the proper order in which it is to make its entrance, or it is quite certain to be brought in at the wrong stage of the repast—if brought at all. But perhaps you have become absorbed in the conversation at table, and so are unobservant of the non-appearance of the greens or other vegetables, till next morning you find them, still in the saucepan, and in a cold and sodden condition.

Thus every detail of each day's "trivial round" has to pass through the mind of the mistress, who is compelled to neglect her work in looking after that of a servant who will not use her own head. One goes to bed at night footsore with running after this terrible servant; and with a head still more wearied by the constant strain of doing all the thinking for every department of the housekeeping. Of course it amounts to much the same as doing the work yourself; and but for "the honour of the thing"—like the Irishman strutting along proudly inside the bottomless sedan-chair, though complaining that he "might as well have walked"—you might as well be without a servant. With South African domestics one realizes indeed the meaning of the word "eye-service"; for not one of them, even the best, knows what it is to be conscientious. They never do a thing right because it *is* right; whatever they think will not be seen is neglected; and they are placidly indifferent as to whether their work is done well or badly, and whether you are pleased or not. One gets so tired of the apathetic yellow or black faces; which never brighten but into a childish laugh, generally at something which is the reverse of a laughing matter for the employer.

Altogether, Phillis is in every way exasperating, and is the great drawback to life on Cape farms. But she is the only kind of servant available; and if you lose patience with her and let her go, you may have to do the whole work of the house yourself, possibly for a week or more, till another, closely resembling her, or perhaps worse, can be found. Therefore, you put up with much, rather than make a change which would involve the training of a raw recruit all unused to English ways, to cleanliness, and to comfort; and indeed hardly acquainted with the rudiments of civilization.

But, unluckily, Phillis herself loves change; it is irksome to her volatile nature to remain long in one place; and accordingly, just as she is becoming used to your ways, and you flatter yourself that you will eventually get her into some sort of training, she flits off, regardless of the inconvenience she may cause. She never tells you in a straightforward manner that she wishes to leave; never gives you time to look out for a substitute; but departs unexpectedly, and always in one of two ways. Most commonly she rises in sudden insubordination, gets up a row of the first magnitude on some trifling pretence, and behaves in so turbulent and uproarious a manner that you are thankful to be rid of her at any cost, and dismiss her then and there; which is just what she wanted.

Or, if she is one of the more peaceful and amiable sort, and has some kindly feeling for the "missis," she leaves the latter in the lurch in a less offensive, though even more heartless manner. She does not *ask* for a holiday, but announces her intention of taking one; faithfully promises to return at the end of four days, and departs, riding astride on a lean and ragged scarecrow of a horse, brought for her by a party of Hottentot friends. It is true she leaves no possessions behind to ensure her coming back; for she never has any luggage, and her wardrobe, being of the scantiest, is all well contained in the handkerchief-bundle which jogs at her side as she trots off. But new chums, fresh from England, and innocent of the ways of the Karroo, are always taken in the first time the trick is played on them; and as the queer-looking cavalcade departs, bearing in its midst the giggling Phillis, no disquieting suspicions cross the mistress's mind. She determines to make the best of it for those four days, and goes bravely to work; either single-handed, or with the so-called help of a small Hottentot girl, who comes just when she chooses—sometimes remaining away a whole day, sometimes arriving in the afternoon when most of the work is done—and who lives so far off that going after her would be useless waste of time. The hours are counted to the time appointed for Phillis's return, but—needless to state—she is never again seen or heard, of; and the victim of her fraud learns by experience that as soon as a servant talks of a holiday it is time to begin the weary search for a successor; never found without plenty of riding about the country, much inquiring on neighbouring and distant farms, and many disappointments.

It is not much use taking English servants to the Karroo; the life is too dull for them, they hear of high wages to be had in Port Elizabeth and other towns, and you never keep them long. The man and wife, both excellent servants, who came with us from England, left us soon after we came up-country; and from that time we had none but coloured servants for house and farm. There was indeed a sudden transformation in our little kitchen; from the quiet, neatly-dressed, white-aproned Mrs. Wells to noisy Hottentot Nancy, in dirtiest of pink cotton, profusely patched with blue and yellow. And the kitchen itself was no less changed than its presiding genius. Now began a time of good hard work for me—for which the usual bringing-up of English girls, followed by years of travel and of hotel life, was not the best of training; and, though I had learned much from Mrs. Wells, I was often sadly at a loss during the first weeks after her departure. No dish, however simple, which I myself was not able to cook, could be cooked by Nancy or any of her successors; all were obliged to see it done at least once before they would attempt it. At this time cookery-books were almost my only literature; and many times a day I sought counsel in a bulky volume wherein recipes and prescriptions, law and natural history, etiquette and the poultry-yard, formed a somewhat startling jumble; and whose index presented, in immediate juxtaposition, such incongruous subjects as liver, lobster, lumbago—marmalade, mayonnaise, measles, meat—shrimps, Shropshire pudding, sick-room, sirloin, sitting-hens, etc. As many despairing sighs as ever fluttered the inky pages of a school lesson-book were breathed over this stout volume. T——, who, after living for years in rougher places than the Karroo, has acquired considerable experience and is a capital cook, helped me out of many a difficulty; and in time I learned to be a tolerably good general servant—which you must be yourself, if you are ever to do any good with Kaffirs or Hottentots. But it was a pity that, when young, instead of many of the things learned at school, I did not acquire what would at this time have made me more independent of servants.

Why is not a knowledge of cooking and house-keeping made a part of every English girl's education? Then, in the event of a colonial life being one day her lot, she is to some extent prepared to encounter the difficulties of that life; while, even if she should marry a millionaire, and be waited on hand and foot for the rest of her days, she is none the worse for possessing the knowledge of how things ought to be done in her house—indeed, every woman who orders a dinner should know something of how it is to be cooked.

Nancy, our first native servant, was also the best we ever had; always bright and good-tempered, and singing over her work in a really charming voice. On the whole she was far more intelligent than most of her race; and we were really sorry when the equestrian family party carried her from our sight, never to return. Then came a succession of "cautions," each worse than her predecessor; and between them all we did indeed, as Mark Twain has it, " know something about woe."

Nancy's immediate successor was in every respect her opposite; idle, impudent, surly, and dishonest; eating as much as two men, but doing no work that was worth anything. She kept yawning all day with loud howls that were most depressing to hear; and when I went into the kitchen I was pretty sure to find her fast asleep, with head and arms on the table.

Our next specimen was a nearly white half-caste, with light-coloured wool, and pale-grey, dead-looking eyes; who always reminded us of one of the horrible, sickly-looking white lizards, so common in Karroo houses. She was half-witted, and most uncanny-looking; with such a ghastly, cold, unsympathetic manner and stony stare that we named her Medusa. We could have picked out many a better servant from the Earlswood Asylum. I was continually trying to think of all the idiotic things she might possibly do, and thus guard against them beforehand; yet she always took me by surprise by doing something ten times more stupid than anything I had dreamed of.

Then came a tall, gaunt old Mozambique negress; in appearance unpleasantly like an ancient Egyptian mummy, and with clothing which looked as though it had been "resurrected" at the same time as herself from a repose of some three thousand years. Only a dirty old black pipe, seldom absent from her lips, savoured, not of the necropolis of Thebes or of Memphis, but of the very vilest Boer tobacco. Besides being an inveterate old thief, she was the exact opposite of a total abstainer; and the frequent " drop too much " in which she indulged was always the occasion for a display of choice language and a reckless destruction of crockery.

But these are enough; suffice it to say that the same types of character ran through a long line of successors, and that, taking them all round, I had about the same amount of trouble with all of them.

T——'s men required almost as much looking after as my women; and, in order to get his herds off to work in good time, it was generally necessary for him to go down himself at sunrise to their little huts, not far from the house, and wake them up. As a rule they were not fond of work; and many were the excuses they would invent in order to avoid it as much as possible. Being " sick " was of course a favourite plea; and, whatever the nature of the complaint from which they professed themselves to be suffering, they were always convinced that a *suppje* (drink) of prickly pear brandy or of " Cape smoke " * would be just the thing to set them right. At one time quite an epidemic of sham sickness broke out; but, as we soon saw through the trick, and knew that our would-be patients were perfectly well, we did not indulge them with their favourite remedy, but determined to make an example. We accordingly treated a very palpable case of shamming with a medicine of our own concoction. We mixed a good saucerful of Gregory's powder and castor oil into

* Boer brandy.

the thickest of paste; and prolonged the agony by making the man eat the stuff with a teaspoon, while we stood sternly on guard, to see that there was no evasion. And then we promised a second dose in the event of the first failing to effect a cure. No need to say that the victim hastened to report himself quite well, and that as long as he remained on the farm he was never "sick" again. The fame of the terrible medicine spread, and we did not hear of much more illness among our men.

This dose was mild, however, in comparison with one of which I have heard, which was prepared by some gentlemen of our acquaintance. They were living in a tent on the Diamond Fields; and for some time had noticed a very rapid diminution of their supply of brandy. Not knowing which of their native servants was the culprit, they resolved to set a trap; and, putting a little croton oil into the brandy-bottle, left the latter in a temptingly prominent position. The next morning one of the servants, a big, stout fellow, was missing; and for ten days nothing was seen or heard of him. When, at the end of that time, he reappeared, he was transformed into such a poor, limp, wasted living skeleton that he could hardly be recognised. He went back to his work without a word; and never again did the brandy-bottle's attractions lure him from the path of honesty.

The best and most hard-working of all our men was a sturdy Zulu, who, both in face and figure, exactly resembled that life-like wooden statue—one of the oldest in the world—which, in the Museum at Cairo, gives us so accurate a portrait of an ancient Egyptian. In looking at it you feel that you can read the character of this man who lived three or four thousand years ago; and know that, although one of the best-tempered of souls, he was as obstinate as Pharaoh himself. Nor were these qualities lacking in his modern fac-simile, the ostrich-herd; whose broad countenance, as he strode after his long-legged charges, bearing, in place of the Egyptian's staff of office, a stout tackey, wore the identical expression which that artist of long ago has caught so well. The good fellow showed a laudable tenacity of purpose in the steady perseverance with which he was putting by all he could save of his wages, and investing the money in cows. With these latter it was his intention to purchase a wife, as soon as a sufficient number could be collected to satisfy the demands of the prospective father-in-law.

A marriage after this fashion, although not quite in accordance with English ideas, has certainly the advantage of inducing good habits in the intending Benedick. In the first place, he learns to economize instead of spending his money on drink. He will, of course, take as many *suppjes* as you like to offer him; but you will never find him going off on the spree for two or three days, and coming back considerably the worse for his outing, as those of his brethren who have not his motive for thrift are too fond of doing. He is altogether a better servant than they, being less independent and more anxious to please. Often, too, he learns to exercise much patience; for, if the girl is pretty, or the father—who always has a keen eye to business—observes that the swain is very devoted, a high price is fixed; and the bridegroom-elect has to work for years, like Jacob for Rachel, till he has accumulated the required number of cows.

Daughters, being such a profitable source of capital, are of course much valued by the parents; to whom, besides, in that sunniest of climates, a large family brings none of the cares and anxieties which it entails on the English labouring-man. The more children a Zulu has, the better he is pleased; the birth of a girl especially being welcomed as gladly as is that of a son among the Jews, and indeed among Orientals generally.

English people settling in the Cape Colony usually start with a strong prejudice in favour of the coloured race. They think them ill-treated, bestow on them a good deal of unmerited sympathy, and credit them with many good qualities which they do not possess. By the time they have been a year or two in the country a reaction has set in; they have discovered that the negro is a fraud; they hate him, and cannot find anything bad enough to say of him. Then a still longer experience teaches them that the members of this childish race are, after all, not so bad, but that they require keeping in their places—treating in fact as you would treat children twelve years old. In intelligence, indeed, they never seem to advance much beyond that age. You must, of course, be just with them; but always keep them at a distance. Above all, never let either men or women servants know that you are pleased with them, or they will invariably presume.

It seems a hard thing to say, but it does not do to be too patient and indulgent; excessive leniency only spoils them, just as it does the Hindoo servants. One of our relatives, a kind and gentle chaplain in India, finding that he was worse waited on than any of his neighbours, and asking his head servant one day why the latter and all his subordinates worked so badly, paid so little attention to orders, etc., received the following candid answer from the man: "Why not *sahib* give plenty stick, and *mem-sahib* call plenty pig? Then we good servants."

A Boer gets much more work out of the natives than an Englishman. The latter is at one time too severe, and at another too lenient; but the Boer's treatment is uniformly just and firm. Perhaps the expression, "like a Dutch uncle," may have originated in the Cape Colony.

The Zulus and Kaffirs are by nature fine, generous characters, comparatively free from dishonesty and untruthfulness; though unfortunately they too soon acquire both these vices, as well as numerous others, when they come in contact with civilization, which in their case certainly seems, as Bret Harte has it, "a failure." On the Diamond Fields the best servants are invariably those who are taken fresh from their kraals; even the fact of their knowing a few words of English being found a disadvantage.

A Zulu is always somewhat of a gentleman, and

possesses a certain code of honour, although to us it seems rather a queer one. For instance, though he will on no account rob his own master, he will not hesitate to steal a sheep from a neighbouring farm, if he should happen to feel inclined for a "big feed"; on which occasion the amount of meat he is able to consume at one sitting is positively alarming. He evidently looks upon the sheep much as Queen Elizabeth is said to have regarded the goose, viz., as a creature of most inconvenient size, "too much for one, but not enough for two." When periodical rations of meat are served out to him he always eats up the whole of his allowance on the first evening, apparently oblivious of the fact that he will have to go without for the rest of the week. And then he subsists, contentedly enough, on mealies, till the joyful time comes for his next good square meal of goat or mutton. He is the happiest and best-tempered of souls, never bearing any animosity, and always ready to forgive; and although he seems incapable of any real attachment to his employers, and is most strangely destitute of all sense of gratitude, one cannot help liking him. Altogether the Zulus are quite the aristocracy of the negro race; and, even at their worst, contrast very favourably with the Hottentots and Bushmen, whose character has hardly a redeeming point, and seems made up of all the lowest and most ignoble qualities.

CHAPTER XI.

HOW WE FARED.

Angora goats—Difficulty of keeping meat—The plague of flies—Rations—Our store—Barter—Fowls—Chasing a dinner—Fowls difficult to rear—Secretary birds as guardians of the poultry-yard—Jacob in the Karroo—He comes down in the world—He dies—Antelopes—A springbok hunt—The Queen's birthday in the Karroo—Colonial dances—Our klipspringer—Superstition about hares—Game birds—*Paauw*—*Knorhaan*—Namaqua partridges—Porcupines—A short-lived pet—Indian corn—Stamped mealies—Wholemeal bread—Plant used for making bread rise—Substitutes for butter—*Priembesjes*—A useful tree—Wild honey—The honey bird—Enemies of bees—Moth in bees' nests—Good coffee—Sour milk.

" How did you live?" is a question we have very often been asked by friends, who, evidently thinking that our fare on that far-away South African farm must necessarily have been of the roughest, and that from a gastronomic point of view we were deeply to be pitied, have been quite surprised to hear that on the whole we lived very well.

To be sure there were drawbacks. In the first place, however simply you may live in the Cape Colony, you cannot possibly live cheaply; for import duties are ruinously heavy, and almost everything, with the exception of meat, has to be imported. Wheat, for instance, has to be brought from Australia; the poor, dry South African colony being quite unable to produce anything like a sufficient supply for its needs. Then, too, green vegetables are very far from being an everyday item in the *menu;* and as for fresh fish, it is a still rarer luxury, indeed throughout all the long, hot summer it is absolutely unobtainable on the farms, and one almost forgets what it is like. Eggs and butter, too, have their long periods, first of excessive and increasing scarcity, and then of entire absence from kitchen and table.

But in the colonies people soon learn to accommodate themselves to circumstances, and contentedly to do without many of the things which in England seemed such necessary adjuncts to daily life. They even become accustomed to a very sad lack of variety in the matter of meat. From one year's end to another merino mutton and Angora goat are almost unchangingly the order of the day; the bill of fare being varied by beef only on those rare occasions, during the very coldest weather, when one of the farmers—having ascertained beforehand that a sufficient number of neighbours are willing to share the meat—is enterprising enough to slaughter an ox. But the difficulties of keeping meat are such that sheep and goats are generally found to be quite large enough; indeed, in the hot weather, they are very much too large, and one is continually wishing that a diminutive race of mutton-producing quadrupeds—say of the size of Skye terriers—were in existence for the benefit of housekeepers in sultry climates. Fortunately you do not get so tired of perpetual mutton as might be expected, and it does not pall on the taste as beef or fowl would do under the same circumstances. As we had only a few sheep, but possessed a flock of several hundred Angoras, our standing dish was, of course, goat. Let not the traveller pity us who on his journeyings—in Southern Europe for instance—has had the misfortune to partake of the tough, stringy, and strongly-flavoured goat's flesh too often iniquitously substituted for mutton by unprincipled hotel-keepers. As different as black from white is that unholy viand from our delicious Angora meat; equal, if not superior, to the best mutton.

The goats are beautiful creatures, with a profusion of long, wavy hair, which is as soft and glossy as the finest silk, and which, in the thoroughbred animals, is of the purest white, and nearly touches the ground. In the evening it is a pretty sight to watch the goats coming down from the mountains, on whose steep and rocky sides they have browsed all day; and where, as they descend, they form a long line of snowy white against the red and green background of the aloes and *spekboom*. It is pleasant, too, to go out to the kraals when the little kids, which all arrive at about the same time, are only a few days old. These goats are prolific creatures, many of them having two, or even three young ones at once. The crowded enclosure is all alive with the merry, noisy little fellows, jumping and scampering about in all directions; and within a few days the number of the flock seems to have almost doubled.

Angora goats are now more profitable than ostriches; although the hair, like feathers, has sadly decreased in value, the price having fallen from 4s. 6d. to 9d. per lb. It seems strange that Angora hair should remain at such a low price; for a costly plush is now made from it, besides very beautiful rugs, many of them perfect imitations of leopard, tiger, and seal-skin—the latter hardly less expensive than real seal.

The morning on which a goat or sheep is killed—especially during very hot weather—ushers in a time of care and anxiety for the frugal housewife. From the moment when the animal expires under the black herd's hands, until the last joint has been brought to table, that meat is an incubus which sits heavy on her soul all day, and occasionally even haunts her dreams at night. She has to wage persistent war against adverse agencies, always in readiness to work its destruction, and, with all her vigilance, too often successfully robbing her of a good portion of it.

First and foremost of all enemies the flies are in the field. As soon as the dead goat or sheep is hung up out of doors, in as cool and shady a place as can be found—though this is by no means saying much—it must instantly be enclosed in a capacious, tightly-tied and carefully-mended bag of mosquito-net, large enough to cover the whole animal. For all around, buzzing excitedly, and eagerly looking out for an opening, however small, through which to squeeze in and do their deadly work, are crowds of big, noisy, determined blue-bottles—though, by the way, if I may be allowed so Irish an expression, in the Karroo these abominations are all green, and—gorgeous as Brazilian beetles—flash like great emeralds in the sunshine.

Phillis, of course, cannot be trusted to go alone to that open-air larder, for she will invariably leave the bag unfastened, even if by her rough handling she does not tear a yawning rent in its side. In the house too, she does her utmost to further the evil designs of the flies, and, if she uses the meat-safe at all, makes a point of leaving it wide open till a host of "green-bottles" has collected inside; when she closes it, leaving them in blissful possession of their prize.

And oh, the house-flies! Truly the plague of flies is in every Karroo home; and, next to the servants, it is the greatest bane of farm life. And what flies they are! Their brethren in other parts of the world, though obnoxious enough, can almost by comparison be called well-behaved. For, except when eatables are about, they do seem to have some idea of keeping to themselves and minding their own business; which latter usually consists in dancing—in the air, and always in the very centre of the room—a kind of quadrille of many intricate figures, the accurate performance of which, holding them completely engrossed, keeps them, for a time at least, out of mischief. But the South African fly has no such resources of his own to keep him amused; consequently he devotes all his energy and the whole of his time to one object—that of making life a burden to the unfortunate human beings on whom he has chosen to quarter himself. Not content with spoiling your appetite at meals by the exhibition of his repulsive little black body in every dish that comes to table, every cup of tea or glass of wine that is poured out—where, whether cooked to death, or yet alive and struggling, it is an equally unwelcome and disgusting sight—he makes it his business to see that throughout the whole day you do not, if he can help it, get one instant's peace. No matter how large the room may be, no place in it will suit him for a perch but just your nose, or the hand which happens to be busily engaged in some operation requiring extreme steadiness, to which a jerk would be fatal; and however many times he is rebuffed, he comes back, with the most unerring and fiendish precision, to exactly the self-same spot, till he has set up a maddening irritation, not only of the skin, but still more of the temper. For he possesses, in the very strongest degree, the quality which led those most observant of naturalists, the ancient Egyptians, to institute the military order of the Fly. A good general, they argued, is like a fly; for, however often he may be repulsed, he always returns persistently to the attack. So they invested the successful leader of their armies with a gold chain, from which, at intervals, hung several large flies of pure, beaten gold, about four inches broad across the closed wings. And in the Cairo Museum a very beautiful chain of this kind is to be seen.

That South African fly was, indeed, the torment of our lives, until one day we made a grand discovery. We found out that he could not stand Keating's insect-powder. If only the smallest grain of it touched any part of his person he was doomed; and in about five minutes would be sprawling helplessly on his back, preparing to quit a world in which he had been so great a nuisance. "Peppering the flies" became a regular institution, the first business of each morning; and in all the rooms, most especially in the kitchen—where the whole atmosphere seemed one vast buzz—the foe would be driven, by the vigorous flapping of a cloth, into the well-sprinkled windows where his fate awaited him. Soon every fly would be dead; and as we gloated over the dustpans full of slain we invoked benedictions on the name of Keating.

By taking care to keep every door and window on the sunny side of the house either closed or covered with fine net, we managed, thanks to this delightful powder, to exist in peace, instead of being given over to the flies like our neighbours; many of whom would calmly submit to any nuisance rather than take a little trouble to get rid of it, and would sit quite contentedly in the midst of a buzzing cloud, with flies popping into their tea one after another, or struggling by dozens in the butter-dish. We found that one of the small bellows made for blowing tobacco-smoke into bee-hives became, when filled with Keating, a very formidable engine of destruction; a couple of puffs, sending the fine powder in all directions, would settle every fly in the room. In fact no one, even in the most tropical of climates, need be troubled with flies, if only this simple remedy is used. If I had but known of its efficacy a few years before, when up the Nile on a *dahabieh* swarming with flies! And if, in that same Egypt, poor Menephtah had only known of it three thousand years ago! Mr. Keating's fortune would have been a colossal one if he had lived then.

But to return to our Angora. As soon as the meat has been cut up it is usually sprinkled very plentifully with salt, and wrapped up for a few hours in the skin; after which the greater portion of it is put into pickle. For in the hot weather only a very small quantity can be eaten unsalted, as it becomes tainted almost at once. Even in strong brine, and with the most careful rubbing and turning, the meat is sometimes quite uneatable on the second day, especially if the weather happens to be thundery. And thunder-storms, when they do come, almost invariably select the time when an animal has just been killed. N.B.—The "pope's eye" must always be carefully taken out as soon as the meat is cut up, or the joint will immediately become tainted.

Where the family is a small one it is a good plan, during the hot weather, to include meat among the men's rations. The herds on the farms receive weekly, as part of their pay, a certain quantity of meal, coffee, sugar, salt, tobacco, etc.; and the store where all these supplies are kept and weighed out on large and business-like scales, looks—with its piles of sacks and packing-cases, its numerous shelves, rows of bottles, tins of preserved meats and other provisions—not at all unlike the general shop of an English village, with a little in the chemist's and tobacconist's line as well.

It is the work of the mistress of the house to give out the rations; and her movements, while manipulating the scales, are watched in a very criticizing and suspicious manner by the black recipients, who always seem terribly afraid that she will give them short weight. In reality she is anxiously and almost nervously careful that every pound she gives them shall be a good one; and if she errs at all it is on their side, never on her own. In the matter of tobacco her heart is especially soft, and the spans she measures off those great coils of dark-brown rope—which surely must be akin to "pigtail tobacco"—are far longer than can be stretched by her hand, or indeed by any hand but that of a giant. But in this, as in every other item of the rations, she is most unjustly and ungratefully suspected of a systematic course of cheating. Sometimes "April" or "August," struck with a sudden bright idea, comes up to the table, and, with many monkey-like gestures, makes a close investigation of the scales and weights; peeping beneath them and looking at them from all sides, to see by what artful device they have been made the means of tricking him. He fails to discover anything; but retires shaking his woolly head dubiously, and as far off as ever from believing in the honesty of his employers.

Sometimes a little barter is carried on, in quite a primitive, old-fashioned way, with Dutchmen travelling by in large waggons drawn by sixteen or eighteen oxen, and often bringing with them very good onions, oranges, *naatjes* or mandarines, nuts, dried peaches and figs—both of which latter are excellent for stewing,—and many other things, which they are glad to exchange on the farms for coffee, sugar, etc. This barter is quite the usual way of doing business in the Karroo; and so many transactions are carried on without the aid of money, that the latter is hardly required, and indeed is seldom seen on the farms. If a man or woman servant comes to do an odd day's work, or a passing workman breaks his journey by staying a couple of days and making himself generally useful, payment is almost always made in meal, coffee, or other articles of food, instead of in money. Copper coins, being universally despised, are not in use; consequently the most trifling service performed, however badly, by one of the coloured race, must be rewarded with no smaller sum than threepence, or—to give it its familiar colonial name—a "tickey."

Fowls, of course, with their obligingly convenient size, are an invaluable boon in the hot weather; and it is a delightful relief when, with an empty larder and consequent light heart, free for a while from the cares and anxieties of the meat, you prolong the respite, and —putting off till to-morrow the slaying of the next four-legged incubus—sacrifice in its stead the noisiest crower, or the most inveterate of the kitchen's feathered intruders. To be sure, hurried, as he is, straight from his last agonies, into the pot or the oven, you cannot expect him to be very tender; but an attempt at hanging him is too likely to result in the sudden discovery that he has hung a little too long, and you have learnt by experience that it is best to eat him at once. And a dessert-spoonful of vinegar, administered half an hour before his execution, will always considerably mitigate his toughness.

Karroo fowls, living a free and active life, are exceedingly agile on their legs, and when their time comes for paying the debt of nature they are by no means easy to catch. But Toto took this duty upon himself, and very jealously asserted his right to perform it. All we had to do was to point out to him the selected victim. Then, with the true collie instinct, he would follow it up, never losing it or making any mistake; and, though it might take refuge in the midst of some twenty or thirty other fowls, Toto would pick it out from among the crowd without an instant's hesitation. And when caught, it was never pounced on roughly, but just quietly held down by the big, gentle paws, from which it would be taken, perfectly unhurt.

How I missed the aid of Toto one day when—he being far away in Kent, and we living near Tangier—I was at my wits' end for a dinner, and trying my hardest to catch a fowl! It was Ramadan—that terrible time when everything goes wrong and everybody is cross—and no wonder; the cruel fast, more strictly kept in orthodox Morocco than it is in most Oriental lands, forbidding the votaries of Islam, from sunrise to sunset, not only to touch food, but even to moisten their parched lips with water—and this in hot weather too! No wonder the sunset gun, instead of being to them the welcome signal for a feast, often finds them so faint and exhausted that they are in no hurry to begin eating. And no wonder, too, that Moorish servants—never very far behind those of South Africa in stupidity—are at this time a greater trial of patience than ever. One does not like to be hard on them, and the minimum of work is given to them; but everything is done so badly that their services might almost as well be dispensed with until the fast is over. Altogether, during this time of woe, the tempers of employers and employed are about equally tried.

Mohammed, our genius, who at the best of times was sure to forget one or more important items of the day's marketing, had on this occasion omitted just everything that was necessary to make a dinner. The bread was there, to be sure, so too were figs and dates; but, all having been put loose into the donkey's panniers and well jolted along the roughest of roads, the eatables had become so hopelessly mixed up with a large dab of native soft soap, bought for the week's washing, that they were only disentangled with difficulty, and the most careful cleansing failed to make them fit for human food. An earthenware jar of honey had been bought; but, being unprovided with a stopper, and left to roll about in the pannier as it pleased, it had poured its contents as a libation along the road, and, when complacently handed to me by Mohammed, was perfectly empty. All the non-edible articles of the day's orders had been carefully remembered, and stowed well away from the soap; but of fish, flesh, or fowl there was no sign. The poor fasting man could not be sent all the way back to Tangier to make good the deficiencies; yet a dinner had to be found somehow for T—— and for a gentleman guest, and with the aid of the servants I set to work to catch one of our own fowls.

But I little knew what I was attempting. Our garden, on the steep slopes of Mount Washington, with its many terraces and walks, flights of rough stone steps, and tangle of luxuriant vegetation, offered so many points of vantage to the active birds, that at the end of half an hour we were all exhausted with running, breathless and giddy with the heat; while the fowls, on the contrary, fresher and livelier than ever, seemed mocking all our efforts to catch them; and in despair I took from its hiding-place a little weapon of defence, provided in view of possible midnight visits from burglarious Moors.

Grasping the revolver in one hand, and with the other treacherously holding out a sieve of barley, I stalked one fowl after another in most unsportsmanlike fashion; inviting the guileless creatures to feed, and then firing at them, sometimes so close that it seemed as if the intended victim must be blown to pieces. But no, there he was, when the smoke cleared away, going off with a triumphant chuckle; wilder and more wary with each unsuccessful shot.

What was to be done? Time was passing; T—— would be coming home hungry by dinner-time, ready for something better than a vegetarian repast; and *some* creature or other—I began to feel that I did not very much care what—had not only to be caught and killed, but also cooked. Reckless and desperate, I began firing indiscriminately, even on my laying hens; but, gladly though I would have killed the best of them, not one could I hit. At last all the hunted birds were in a state of the wildest excitement; none were in sight, and an agonized chorus of cackling resounded from all parts of the garden, as if the largest and most venomous of snakes had been seen. Flinging down the revolver in disgust, I meditated the crowning baseness of snatching the poor old sitting hen from the eggs on which she had quietly sat throughout the commotion, when—joyful sight—Mohammed, who had mysteriously vanished, suddenly reappeared, triumphantly holding up by the neck a plucked fowl. It was but a poor, scraggy, spidery-looking thing, all legs and wings, and with an appearance of having kept Ramadan no less strictly than the Moorish owners from whose hut the poor fellow—anxious to retrieve his fault—had brought it. But it was something off which to dine; and never was the fattest Christmas turkey more welcome than was its timely appearance.

The rearing of fowls in South Africa is attended with endless difficulties and discouragements. Frequent epidemics of the fatal disease known as "fowl-sickness" decimate the poultry-yard, which, at the best of times, and with all care, can never be kept sufficiently stocked to supply the needs of the hot weather. Every possible foe of the gallinaceous tribe abounds in the Karroo; snakes invade the hen-house, and the blackmail which they levy on the eggs always amounts to what the

Americans call "a large order;" birds of prey of many different sorts are constantly sailing over head, with sharp eyes on the look-out for opportunities of plunder; and jackals, wild cats, lynxes—or, as the Dutch call them, *rooikats*—and numerous other four-legged freebooters pounce at night on those hens foolish enough to make their nests far from the comparative safety of the house; the occasional discovery, in some distant bush, of a collection of empty eggshells and a heap of drifted feathers proclaiming what has been the fate of some long-missing hen or turkey.

Altogether, the poultry-keeper's troubles are considerably multiplied by the surpassing imbecility of the Karroo hens, which have no idea of taking care of themselves, and, like the ostriches, stoutly oppose all efforts made for their own welfare and that of their offspring. Their insanely erratic conduct during sitting causes by far the larger proportion of nests to come to nothing; and when they have succeeded in hatching a few chickens, they look as if they did not quite know what to do with them.

Secretary birds are sometimes taught to be very useful guardians of the poultry-yard, especially against aerial enemies,—the long-legged, solemn-looking creature stalking about all day among his feeble-minded charges, with much consciousness of his own importance. He is accused of now and then taking toll in the shape of an occasional egg or young chicken—the latter being of course bolted, anaconda-fashion; but his depredations are not extensive, and one tolerates them as one does those of the courier who, though himself not entirely above suspicion, takes good care that his master is robbed by no one else.

Our secretary, Jacob, whose education had been neglected in youth, refused to make himself useful as a protector of the poultry-yard. His character, never the most amiable, deteriorated rapidly after we brought him up-country, carefully packed for the long railway journey; the numerous bandages in which he was swathed to secure his long, slender legs from breakage giving him—but for his protruding, vulture-like head—the appearance of a gigantic ibis-mummy. Our first plan of making him trudge on foot along the road with the Walmer caravan of ostriches was given up, as we felt sure that, with his already-mentioned "cussedness," he would give more trouble to the herds than all the rest of the troop together, and either get a knock on the head to settle him, or else escape, never to be heard of again. At any rate, he would be quite sure not to arrive at his destination.

Poor Jacob did not flourish in the Karroo, where kittens were scarce, and where no butcher's cart brought daily and ample supplies for his colossal appetite; and an existence in which fresh meat was so rare a luxury must have been for him a kind of perpetual Lent.

With much resentment and plainly-expressed disgust at his reverse of fortune, he found himself obliged, late in life, to pick up a living for himself, and would wander dejectedly about the country for miles round, in search of the fat, succulent locusts, the frogs, small snakes, lizards, and mice on which he fed. The latter he caught in a most ingenious manner. Walking up to a bush wherein he knew a mouse was concealed, he would strike a violent blow with his wing on one side; then, as the startled animal ran out in the opposite direction, Jacob would make a lightning-like pounce, and bring down his murderous foot with unerring aim. On the whole he did not fare badly; but of course, after his luxurious bringing-up among the fleshpots of Walmer, it was but natural that he should object to working for a living.

Even in prosperous days he loved to look ill-used, and no comic actor could have better represented the character of an ill-tempered old man nursing a grievance than did the well-fed Jacob croaking under the windows in mendacious pretence of starvation; but now his part was so absurdly overacted that it became a burlesque. Nature at the same time assisted him in his make-up for the part, and, moulting and tail-less, with bald head and general out-at-elbows appearance, he looked indeed the seediest and most disreputable of old beggars. At the best of times he looked like a wicked old man, but now—no longer a sleek, well-clothed old sinner—he seemed to have degenerated into a ruined gambler, going rapidly to the dogs. Whenever there was a big rain he would come and stand in front of the windows, wet through and shivering ostentatiously, with the water running in a little stream from the tip of his hooked bill, giving him the appearance of one of the ugly gargoyles on an ancient cathedral. Obstinately refusing to come under cover, or even to keep himself comparatively dry by squatting under the kraal hedge, he would stand for hours out in the rain, looking ill-used and woe-begone; a picture of squalid, unlovely poverty.

We really pitied the old bird, and regretted our inability to give him daily the fresh meat which, in spite of frequent disappointments, he never failed to claim, noisily and importunately, as his right. He would come walking excitedly into the kitchen or bedroom, clamouring, with all the persistence of Shylock, for his pound of flesh; or would run after Wells as the latter went to chop wood, knocking against his legs, getting in his way to attract attention, and keeping up his horrible clock-work noise, till we wondered that that most patient and even-tempered of men, with the hatchet so handy, was not provoked into chopping off his head.

At last a long drought set in, and poor Jacob came still further down in the world; for, as the ground hardened, and vegetation dried up, the "mice and rats and such small deer" of the *veldt* became more scarce, and he had to travel longer distances in search of his prey. We did all we could for him, and kept quite a battery of mousetraps constantly set for his benefit; but, compared with his enormous demands, all we could give him was but as a drop in the ocean, and we felt that he despised us for our meanness. He grew daily more morose, and would vent his ill-humour by picking quarrels with the dogs and other creatures about the place, especially with a pretty little *duyker* antelope. This gentle and timid little favourite—a short-lived pet, which, wandering one day too far from home, was shot by a Boer in mistake for a wild animal—was several times attacked so savagely by the vengeful Jacob, that, if Wells had not beaten off the assailant, the little buck would have been killed. Fortunately Jacob, when excited, always made such a horrible noise, that we could hear when a battle was going on, and rush to the rescue. As the drought continued Jacob took to wandering further and further afield, coming to the house only on rare occasions, until at last he became almost like a wild bird; and we have little doubt that these roving propensities, at a time when water was only to be found at the few-and-far-between homesteads, led at last to the poor old fellow's death from thirst—a sad end for one of the most comical, if not the best-tempered of our pets.

Game, of course, forms a very welcome break in the monotony of constant goat and mutton. The antelopes, though by no means plentiful, are all excellent eating, and afford good sport. The graceful springbok, one of the most common, is capable of becoming very tame; and, with its slender limbs and bright-coloured, variegated coat, it is, but for its rather goat-like face, one of the prettiest of pet animals. On a large neighbouring farm the springbok were preserved, and now and then the somewhat even tenour of Karroo existence would be enlivened by a hunt, sometimes of several days' duration. The Queen's birthday is a favourite occasion for these festive gatherings; and from far and wide, some from distances of two or three days' journey, travelling on horseback or in roomy American spiders and carts capable of accommodating large family parties, visitors arrive in rapid succession, till the house—which at these times seems endowed with even more than the usual elasticity of the hospitable colonial homes—appears like some large hotel overflowing with guests. In the extensive plains surrounding the house the chase goes on merrily throughout the whole day; many of the hunted bucks being observable from the verandah as they speed lightly along, with a bounding motion suggestive of india-rubber balls, and with the sunlight flashing upon the ridge of long white bristles along the back, invisible when the animal is in repose, but erected when it is startled.

In the evening the trophies of the battue, sometimes amounting to the number of thirty, are laid side by side in close ranks upon the ground in front of the house, forming a noble display. The day's adventures are recounted, with much chaffing of the by no means few who have been bucked off or who have otherwise come to grief; T—— on one occasion bearing off the palm as the butt of the most pitiless jokes, his horse, declining the superadded weight of a fine buck, having deposited him on his head, in which acrobatic posture he is reported to have remained standing long enough to give rise to much speculation among the onlookers as to whether he intended finally to land on face or back.

By-and-by the silence of the *veldt* is further broken by the unaccustomed sound of fireworks, and of loud cheers for the Queen from the stout lungs of her lieges beneath the Southern Cross; then come some capital theatricals and a dance, the latter prolonged a good way into the small hours of the morning. There are no better dancers anywhere than the Cape colonists; they are of course passionately fond of the art in which they so much excel; and thus, when a large and merry party have collected—not without considerable difficulties, and at the cost of the longest and roughest of journeys—they naturally like to keep it up as long as possible, and it is by no means an uncommon thing on these occasions for people not to go to bed at all, but for the morning sun, peeping in under the vines of the verandah, to find the dance still in full swing.

The Cape negroes, too, are all born dancers; and it needs but a few notes scraped on a fiddle or wheezed on an asthmatic accordeon to set a whole company of even the roughest and most uncouth Hottentots waltzing in perfect time, and in a quiet and almost graceful manner, strangely out of keeping with their ungainly forms.

Rarest among the antelopes is the klipspringer,[*] which is called the chamois of South Africa, and which, both in appearance and habits, closely resembles the Alpine animal. Its flesh, which is short and dark, with a flavour very like that of duck, is by far the best of all the venison; and its pretty coat is a marvel of soft-

[*] *Oreotragus saltatrix.*

ness and lightness, each hair being a wide tube as thick as a hedgehog's bristle, but soft as a feather. In spite of its light weight, this curious coat is wonderfully thick and durable, and saddle-cloths made from it are simply perfection.

A little klipspringer was brought to us, so young that for the first few weeks it was fed with milk from a baby's bottle. It soon grew tame, and it was very pretty to see the miniature chamois trotting confidingly about the house, always on the extreme tips of those natural alpenstocks, its little pointed feet. These tiny ferules, all four of which would have stood together on a penny-piece, were evidently capable of giving a firm foothold even in the most impossible places. This little creature was one of our unlucky pets—by far the most numerous class in the collection,—and our hope of taking him to England, where he would have enjoyed the proud distinction of being the first of his kind ever imported, was doomed to disappointment. Whether it is really the fact, as one is always told in South Africa, that this buck cannot live in captivity, or whether an inveterate habit of eating the contents of the waste-paper basket, with an impartial relish for printed and written matter, shortened the life of our specimen, I do not know; but rapid consumption set in, and the pathetic, almost human attacks of coughing were so distressing to witness that it was a relief when the poor little patient succumbed.

Then, also among the smaller antelopes, there are the duyker and stenbok. Both these pretty little bucks make forms like hares, and the stenbok, a wee thing very little larger than a hare, is not unlike that animal in flavour.

As for "poor Wat" himself, the uncanny reputation which in all lands he seems so unjustly to have acquired is here intensified; and among Boers, Kaffirs, and Hottentots he is the object of so superstitious a dread that none will venture to eat him. His inoffensive little body is firmly believed to be tenanted by the spirits of dead-and-gone relatives and friends; and even Phillis, by no means a dainty feeder—to whom a good epidemic of fowl-sickness is a welcome harvest, and the sudden and fatal apoplectic fit of the fattest turkey the occasion of a right royal feast and long-remembered red-letter day,—is indignant and insulted if you offer her what is left of a particularly delicious jugged hare. To have lent a hand in cooking the unholy beast was sacrilege enough, but there her not over-sensitive conscience draws the line. Most uncanny of all the hares is the *springhaas*. This creature, with disproportionately long hind-legs and kangaroo-like mode of progression, is never seen in the daytime, and can only be shot on moonlight nights.

The best game birds of the Karroo are those of the bustard tribe. Of the great bustard, or *paauw*, there are two kinds; one, a gigantic bird, sometimes weighing as much as seventy pounds. In hunting the *paauw*— as in stalking the wily mosquito—your first and special care must be not to let the object of your chase see you looking at him. With well-acted unconsciousness, and eyes carefully turned in any direction but towards the spot where the *paauw* squats in the grass, you ride round and round him in an ever-lessening circle, until you get within range. Then you jump off, make a run at him, and fire.

A smaller bustard, with beautifully-variegated plumage, is about the size of a large fowl. His Dutch name of *knorhaan*—which may be translated "scolding cock," or "growling fowl"—is very justly bestowed on him to express his exceeding noisiness, and I do not think that throughout the whole length and breadth of the bird kingdom there exists such another chatterer. What a start he gives you sometimes when, on a brisk ride or drive through the *veldt*, you approach his hiding-place, and suddenly, before you have had time to see his slender dark neck and head peering out above the low bush, he springs up with a deafening clamour, as of a dozen birds instead of one; and, unless silenced by a shot, he continues his harsh, discordant noise, apparently without once stopping for breath, until his swift wings have borne him far away out of hearing. A whole chorus of blackbirds, suddenly disturbed from revels among ripe fruit, would be nothing in comparison with him.

The quaint, old-fashioned-looking little *dikkop*, smallest of the bustard tribe, is, in the opinion of epicures, the best of all. In the bustards the position of the white and dark meat is reversed, the flesh being dark on the breast and white on the legs. They possess certain feathers which are invaluable to the makers of flies for fishing.

Of partridges there are two kinds, the red-wing and grey-wing, the latter being found only on the mountains. The beautiful little "Namaqua partridges," which come in flights, are in reality a kind of grouse. It is a pretty sight when, at sundown, these neatest and most delicately-plumaged of little birds collect in large numbers to drink at the dams.

Of some of our queer dishes, such as *consomme d'autruche* and the mock-turtle afforded by the gigantic tortoises of the *veldt*, I have already spoken. Now and then, too, when a porcupine was killed, we would follow the example of the Algerian Arabs, and dine sumptuously off its flesh, which was not unlike English pork with extra-good crackling.

A baby porcupine, which was taken alive and unhurt, was for some weeks an amusing addition to the menagerie; and many were our regrets when—just as he was getting tame and friendly—he fell a victim to an unexpected cold night, against which, in his little box out of doors, we had ignorantly left him insufficiently protected. At first his temper, which was decidedly of the kind usually described as "short," gave us much amusement; and, when irritated by our approach, he would stamp his little feet, wheel round impetuously, and come charging at us backwards, with all his quills erect, and an absurd expression of energetic pugnacity depicted, not only on his small, snub-nosed countenance, but throughout the whole of his bristling body.

Unfortunately, "the pig with the sticks on his back,"

as the Kaffirs call the porcupine, is the worst of gardeners; and provoking indeed is the devastation wrought by his omnivorous appetite among potatoes, carrots, parsley, pumpkins, water-melons, and indeed all other plants which, in our most thankless of kitchen gardens, are grown and irrigated with such infinite toil and difficulty.

The crop which best repays cultivation in that arid soil is Indian corn. This most wholesome and nourishing food is much more suitable for hot climates than oatmeal, as it possesses none of the heating properties of the latter; and, although in one form or another it is a standing dish at nearly every meal in a Karroo house, one never tires of it. The nicest way of preparing it is in the form called "stamped mealies." The ripe yellow grains of the Indian corn are moistened and placed in a large and massive wooden mortar, generally consisting of the stump of a tree hollowed out. (The centre of an old waggon-wheel did duty very effectually as our mealie-stamper.) Then, with a heavy wooden pestle, they are bruised just sufficiently to remove the yellow husks, though not enough to break up the corn itself, as in the case of the American hominy. After a long and gentle boiling the mealies are as tender as young peas, and it is difficult for a stranger to believe that they have not been cooked in milk.

It would be a good thing if those who make it their study to provide cheap and nourishing food for the starving poor of London and other over-populated towns would try stamped mealies. The small cost of the Indian corn and the simple and easy manner of its preparation would enable it to be supplied in large quantities; and the really excellent dish, if it once became known in England, could not fail to be popular. In some parts of South Africa the natives live almost entirely on Indian corn, especially the Zulus, than whom no finer race of men could be found.

If, among all the different competitions now set on foot, there were one for bread-makers of all countries, surely the Dutchwomen of the Karroo would bear away the prize for their delicious whole-meal bread, leavened with sour dough and baked in large earthenware pots. It is beautifully sweet and light; and as Phillis's bread—besides containing almost as plentiful a sprinkling of flies as there are currants in a penny bun—is in every way more often a failure than a success, it is as well for the lady settler promptly on arrival to take a lesson from some neighbouring *vrouw*, and herself to undertake the bread-making.

While on the subject of whole-meal bread, why is it that in England the nutritious, flinty part of the grain is almost invariably taken out and made into macaroni or used for other purposes, while the bread is made of flour from which all the goodness has been refined away? If whole-meal bread is ordered of the English baker, he throws a handful of bran into this same flour; and the brown loaf looks tempting enough, but both it and the white one are alike tasteless and insipid, and destitute of nutritious qualities. What is really wanted for good bread is just simply the entire contents of the grain, as nature, who after all knows best, has given it to us.

Better than sour dough, yeast, and all the baking-powders in the world is a preparation made by the Kaffir women from a curious and rather rare little plant which grows in the Karroo. This plant is almost all root, the small portion which peeps above the ground consisting only of a few tight clusters of small, shiny knobs, of a dull leaden colour. There is nothing like it for making bread rise; but it is most difficult to get any of it, as the Kaffir women, besides being too lazy to relish the work of preparing it, which is a long and tedious business, make a mystery and a secret of it: no servant will own to understanding it, and somehow one never gets to see the whole process, and is only shown certain stages of it, one of which consists in the hanging up of the substance for a while in a bag exposed to the air, during which time it increases enormously in bulk, in a manner which seems almost miraculous.

Butter being so rare a luxury in the Karroo, a number of different substances have to be pressed into the service during long droughts to supply its place, such as lard, dripping, etc., and, for the table, the fat from the huge tails of sheep somewhat resembling those of Syria, though not, like the latter, kindly provided with little carts on which to drag the cumbersome weight. English jams, of course, like all other imported provisions, are ruinously expensive; and it is a pity that the Natal preserves, plentiful as are both fruit and sugar in that most fertile of lands, are hardly less extravagant in price. But very good home-made jams can be obtained from the Cape gooseberry—a kind of small tomato, enclosed in a loose, crackling bag much too large for it; also from *priembesjes* (pronounced "primbessies"), a delicious wild fruit which grows on small trees along the lower slopes of the mountains. These trees only bear biennially; and, as if exhausted by the lavish profusion of fruit yielded each alternate season, produce nothing in the intermediate year. The pretty fruit, resembling a small, semi-transparent cherry, is at first completely enclosed in such a tight-fitting case that it looks like a soft, velvety green ball. As the fruit ripens this green covering divides in half, and gradually opens wider and wider, disclosing the vivid scarlet within. Amid the prevailing stiffness and sombreness of Karroo vegetation the pretty, rounded outline of these trees, and their bright, glossy, dark foliage—forming an effective background for the jewel-like fruit as it peeps from the delicate pale-green cases in all different stages of expansion—afford a pleasing contrast.

In search of *priembesjes* we made many delightful expeditions on horseback to the foot of the mountains; sitting in our saddles close to the trees and picking from our animals' backs, T—— occasionally standing up like a circus-rider to reach the higher boughs. Our horses became quite accustomed to the work, and, moving into the exact spot desired, would stand motionless as long as we chose while we filled our baskets.

The fruit is slightly acid and very refreshing; and the preserve, not unlike cherry jam, well repays the trouble of making, which is considerable, the enormous stones being quite out of proportion to the size of the fruit, and very difficult to separate from the pulp. Even these stones, however, possess their good qualities, and contain a delicate little kernel, as nice a nut as you could wish to eat, from which an excellent oil can be pressed. Then, too,—no small recommendation in the eyes of ladies,—they make the most delightful beads, being just soft enough to pierce with a good strong needle, though not so soft as to shrivel up afterwards. They are of all different shades of rich brown, and, when threaded into necklaces, remind one of the old Arab rosaries in Cairo, made from the "Mecca seeds," and rubbed to a brilliant polish by devout Mohammedan thumbs. Jam, beads, oil, and nuts! Surely a tree with such numerous and varied ways of making itself useful to humanity seems quite worthy to have figured in the pages of "The Swiss Family Robinson."

The wild honey of the Karroo is generally very good, though some is occasionally found to which unwholesome flowers have imparted their evil qualities. If, for instance, "where the bee sucks" there is much euphorbia-blossom, the honey is pungent and burns the tongue. Sometimes it is even poisonous.

A most useful volunteer assistant in the taking of bees' nests is the honey-bird, an insignificant-looking little brown fellow who seems possessed of an almost uncanny amount of intelligence. Well does he know that old tree or that hole in the ground where there is a goodly store of the sweet food into which he is longing to plunge his bill; but, unfortunately, he cannot get it out for himself, and must needs call in the aid of a human ally to take the nest. So he wanders hither and thither, and, hailing the first person he meets, flies close up to him, chirping and calling loudly to attract attention, and behaving altogether in such a confidingly familiar and impudent manner that strangers unaccustomed to his ways would take him for a tame bird escaped from his cage. If you refuse to follow him he gets very angry, and shows his impatience by flying backwards and forwards, chirping excitedly; but if his guidance is accepted—although he may give you a very long, rough walk—he will lead you without fail to the nest.

As soon as the spot is reached he changes his note; and, while his featherless partner secures the prize, he sits close by, watching the proceedings with intense interest, and waiting for his share of the plunder. The natives are always superstitiously careful to leave him a liberal portion; for they credit him with a very vindictive disposition, and say that if any one is base enough to refuse him his well-earned reward, he will revenge himself on the next person he meets, however innocent the latter may be, and, under pretence of taking him to a bees' nest, will lure him to the lair of a leopard, the hole of a venomous snake, or some other equally undesirable spot.

One day T——, on a long homeward ride, was waylaid by one of these birds, which, taking him under his protection in the usual business-like and patronizing manner, led him by a most roundabout route, and at last, with many fussy demonstrations, conducted him triumphantly to our own beehive, close to the house. Then he perched on a little bush from whence he could contemplate the bees; and T—— called me out to look at him as he sat chirping, immensely contented with himself, and scolding us loudly for our neglect of duty.

Among the numerous enemies of bees the pretty bird called the bee-eater is one of the most destructive; and wherever there is a hive or a nest several of these birds are almost sure to be seen, darting about swiftly and catching the poor little insects on the wing. A large kind of hornet is also continually on the watch for bees, which he slays apparently out of pure spite; and last, though by no means least, a horrid little red scorpion-like creature invades the hive itself, killing many of the inmates.

A large moth resembling the death's-head often takes up its abode in bees' nests, betraying its presence by a peculiar plaintive sound, and apparently living in a perfectly friendly and peaceful manner with its hosts. The natives, however, and indeed also many of the colonists, stand in great awe of it, as they imagine it to be possessed of a most deadly sting. Throughout the whole country one hears accounts of men, oxen, etc., being killed by this terrible moth; and T——, wishing to investigate the matter and find out whether there were any truth in the tale, sent several specimens to England, where, on examination by an authority on entomology, they all proved to be destitute of stings.

You never get a bad cup of coffee in South Africa. That unholy ingredient, chicory, with which people in England persist in making their coffee undrinkable, is never used, and all, even on the roughest of farms, seem to understand the secret of preparing good coffee, which, after all, needs but the observance of a very simple rule; *i.e.*, never to roast or grind more at a time than is required for immediate use. The Dutch *vrouw's* coffee would be perfection if she would only refrain from making it the medium by which to express the depth of her kindly feelings towards her guests, and turning it to a sickly syrup by adding sugar in the proportion of Falstaff's "intolerable deal of sack." And Phillis, however hopelessly ignorant she may be on all other points of cookery, prepares the huge bowl of *café au lait*, which, in accordance with colonial custom, she brings to your bedside in the early morning, in a manner which partially atones for her multitude of sins.

Yet people at home do not seem to realize that coffee, if kept even for a little time after it is roasted, and—worse still—after it is ground, completely loses its flavour. As a rule they buy it ready ground, in large quantities, and keep it for weeks in the house and under such circumstances it is no wonder that even in the best hotels the coffee is not fit to drink, and that too often, but for the only flavour left in it

—that of the acrid chicory with which it has been bountifully doctored—it might be taken for weak tea. And yet there is no better "pick-me-up" after a long walk or tiring day's work, nothing more warming and comforting on a cold day, than a cup of really good coffee. Such, for instance, as you get in any of the numerous Arab *cafés* in Algiers; a tiny cup of which, hardly larger than an egg-cup, does you more good than a glass of port wine. Indeed, wherever coffee is really well made—as in France and Spain—it does extensively take the place of intoxicating drinks; and it would be a good thing if in England, and especially among our poorer classes, this splendidly nutritious substance—food no less than drink—were as much used as it is abroad. The coffee-house where well-made, unadulterated coffee might be obtained would be a formidable rival to the gin-palace. As it is, however, the art of making coffee—if ever possessed at all in England—has been so completely lost that the increasing disuse of the beverage is no matter of surprise.

Angora milk is excellent with coffee, but, though abundant at times, it is hardly to be obtained at all during droughts; and for months you have to be contented with Swiss milk. The Boers and Kaffirs think fresh, sweet milk very unwholesome; a Dutchwoman never gives her child anything but sour milk to drink, and the Kaffirs always keep their milk in large gourds which have the property of rapidly turning it sour.

CHAPTER XII.

KARROO BEASTS, BIRDS AND REPTILES.

>Leopard drowned in a well—Baboons—Egyptian sacred animals on Cape farms — "Adonis" — A humiliating retreat — A baby baboon—Clever tricks performed by baboons—Adonis as a *Voorlooper*—A four-handed pointsman—Sarah—A baboon at the Diamond Fields—Adonis's shower-bath—His love of stimulants—His revengeful disposition—Pelops the dog-headed—Horus — *Aasvogels* — Goat-sucker—The butcher-bird's larder—Nest of the golden oriole—The kapok bird—Snakes in houses—A puff-adder under a pillow—Puff-adder most dangerous of Cape snakes—Cobras—*Schaap-sticker*—Ugly house-lizards—Dassie-adder—The dassie the coney of Scripture—Stung by a scorpion—Fight between tarantula and centipede—Destructive ants—The *Aardvaark*, or ant-bear—Ignominious flight of a sentry — Ant-lion — Walking-leaves — The Hottentot god—A mantis at a picnic.

ALTHOUGH the elephant and lion are now no longer found in the Karroo, there still remain a good number of leopards, or, as the colonists, in calm defiance of natural history, persist in calling them, "tigers." These animals, by the way, seem fated at both ends of the Dark Continent to be the victims of a misnomer, and in Algeria rejoice in the name of *panthère*. Though the South African leopards are now following the example of the larger and more formidable game, and gradually retreating before the advance of man, it is not many years since three or four of them might be seen drinking together at night from the dam close to the Dutch house now transformed into the homestead of Swaylands. Even now, in the hills overlooking the Karroo, there are more of them about than the farmer likes; and sheep, calves, colts and young ostriches are occasionally killed by them.

One day, riding up to a well in an out-of-the-way part of the farm, we found that a magnificent full-grown leopard had fallen in and drowned himself. There he was, floating on the surface of the water only five feet below where we stood; his large body extended across the whole diameter of the well, and on the steep but rough and unbricked sides of the latter we could see the traces of his desperate though unavailing struggles to climb out. Unfortunately, the weather being very hot, his beautiful skin was already spoilt; and we rode home regretting the lovely rug "off our own farm," which we might have displayed to admiring friends at home if we had but found him one day earlier.

A wounded leopard is a very dangerous customer. One of our neighbours, an old hunter, bears many scars in remembrance of severe injuries received long ago in following up one of these animals which he had shot. The encounter was a terrible one, nearly costing the colonist his life.

Next to the leopard in ferocity comes the baboon. He is a big, deep-voiced, sturdy fellow; his short, gruff bark is as dog-like as his head, and there is no doubt that he is identical with the dog-headed ape of ancient

Egypt. Indeed, all the sacred animals and birds of Egyptian mythology, and many of the other creatures which are depicted in so life-like a manner on the walls of Nile temples and tombs, are to be found at this day in South Africa. Anubis the jackal; the grey ibis, now extinct in Egypt, but common enough in the Cape Colony, and—audacious insult to that learned god to whom he was sacred—irreverently and absurdly named by the colonials "oddida;" the hawk Horus, with just the same plump little body, round baby-face, and delicately-tinted plumage of softest French grey and white which you see again and again in those comical, toy-like little wooden images in the museum at Cairo; the wild geese, with the identical curious markings of those which, in the oldest picture in the world, may be seen in that same museum; the scarab, rolling his unwieldy ball with Atlas-like efforts;—all these are at home on the Karroo farms.

Cynocephalus, indeed, was very much more at home at Swaylands than we liked, and would often frighten the ostriches into a wild state of panic, with the usual inevitable result of broken legs. On mountain excursions you frequently hear his surly bark, and sometimes see him looking out defiantly at you from behind rock or bush, where possibly you have disturbed him in the midst of an exciting lizard-hunt, or careful investigation of loose stones in search of the centipedes, scorpions and beetles hidden beneath. These creatures, uninviting though they appear to us, are among his favourite dainties, and he catches them with wonderful dexterity. In the silence of night his voice is so distinctly audible from the homestead that you would imagine him to be close by, though in reality he is far off in one of the kloofs of the mountains. One night, as we strolled up and down near the house, enjoying the bright moonlight, a loud chorus of distant baboons to which we were listening was suddenly interrupted, evidently by the spring of a hungry leopard, the moment's silence being followed by the agonized and prolonged yells of the victim.

Now and then Cynocephalus, or, as the Boers ironically call him, "Adonis," gets too troublesome, and war has to be carried into his camp. Of no avail against *him* are those neat little strychnine pills, enclosed in tempting pieces of fat, by means of which Anubis is so successfully sent to his account. No vegetable poison has the slightest effect on the baboon's iron constitution, and indeed, if there exists any poison at all capable of killing him, it is quite certain that with his superior intelligence he would be far too artful to take it; and when the fiat for his destruction has gone forth a well-organized attack has to be made on him with dogs and guns. He can show fight, too, and the dogs must be well trained and have the safety of numbers to enable them to face him; for in fighting he has the immense advantage of hands, with which he seizes a dog and holds him fast while he inflicts a fatal bite through the loins. Indeed, for either dog or man, coming to close quarters with Adonis is no trifling matter.

One of our friends, travelling on horseback, came upon a number of baboons sitting in solemn parliament on some rocks. He cantered towards them, anticipating the fun of seeing the ungainly beasts take to their heels in grotesque panic; but was somewhat taken aback on finding that—far from being intimidated by his approach—they refused to move, and sat waiting for him, regarding him the while with ominous calmness. The canter subsided into a trot, and the trot into a sedate walk—and still they sat there; and so defiant was the expression on each ugly face that at last the intruder thought it wisest to turn back and ride ignominiously away.

A Dutch boy—one of a family temporarily camping in their own waggon on the farm, and employed by T——, rambling one day in one of the far-off kloofs of the mountains, came near the haunt of a party of baboons. Though an occasional bark broke the stillness, only one of the animals was in sight, and that a little one, probably left alone for a while during the mother's search for food. With the baby baboon in his arms the boy was soon speeding at his best pace down the mountain; and, if fortune had but favoured his enterprise as it deserved, what a delightful "new chum" would that day have been added to our collection of animals! But too soon the whole troop of baboons, missing their youngest hope, were in full pursuit of the robber, on whom they gained so rapidly, and with gestures so unmistakeably portending mischief, that young Piet was only too glad to drop his prize and run for his life.

The baboon stands in no awe of women; he seems quite aware of their inferiority, in point of strength and courage, to the sterner sex, and despises them accordingly. At one place near Graaff-Reinet the women never dared to go and fetch water unless accompanied by men; for the baboons, which were very numerous, would always chase and threaten any daughter of Eve who ventured, without masculine escort, near their haunts.

Baboons captured in babyhood and brought up in human society are capable of becoming extremely tame. Like all other very intelligent animals, they vary much in disposition, a docile and tractable one soon learning to perform many clever tricks, and being an amusing companion, though too often a mischievous one. A gentleman at Willowmore owned two large, splendidly-trained performing baboons, which would have made the fortune of any circus-proprietor. They would together enact a series of complicated tricks, each going through his allotted part without a mistake. Both were most attentive and obedient to orders, and never by any chance would "Joe" so far forget his duty as to respond to the command given to "Jim," or *vice versâ*.

Occasionally, too, Adonis—who cannot, even by his best friends, be called ornamental—is taught to make himself useful; he has in several instances been seen filling the post of *voorlooper* to the waggons of travelling Boers, acquitting himself on the whole quite as creditably as his Hottentot fellow-servants. And at one railway station in the colony a baboon was for a long time employed to work the points. The man in charge of the latter—having in a railway accident lost one arm and part of the remaining hand—had taught the ape to move the levers. This he did most cleverly with three of his powerful hands, using one of the hinder ones; and the fact of the novel pointsman retaining his situation makes it evident that his duties were satisfactorily performed.

On the occasion of a raid with dogs and guns on the baboons infesting a friend's farm, one of the animals killed was the mother of a very young infant. When the captors came up to the spot they found the poor little creature crying piteously as it clasped the trunk of the tree beneath which lay its dead parent. They took it home, and our friend, a great lover of animals, was successful in rearing it. "Sarah," a gentle, amiable character, soon became a great favourite, and her comical ways were a source of constant amusement to her human friends. At the word of command she would stand erect, with her arms behind her, and her mouth wide open to catch the pieces of potato, etc., which were thrown into it; and when told to open "wider! wider!" she would distend her jaws almost to the point of breaking.

Of course she was occasionally—what member of the ape tribe is not?—the victim of practical jokes. One day her favourite dish, pumpkin, was presented to her, and, all-unconscious of the treachery which lurked within, she applied herself with gusto to her dinner, which, unlike most of her tribe, she always preferred to eat direct from the dish without the intervention of her fingers. Alas! between two of those succulent slices of pumpkin cruel hands had spread a thick layer of mustard; and poor Sarah, eating greedily, soon experienced direful results on tongue, palate, throat, and eyes. She knew at once that she had been tricked; and never were contempt and indignation better expressed than by the lordly manner in which she kicked away the dish with all its remaining contents. After which she retired, much offended, to her bed, from whence she did not emerge for a long time.

On another occasion poor Sarah was made the subject of a still more unkind practical joke. She dearly loved sweets, which were often given to her wrapped up in a multitude of papers, one inside the other. It was amusing to watch the patient and deliberate manner in which she would unfold each paper in turn, taking the greatest care never to tear one, and proceeding with all the caution of a good Mohammedan fearful of inadvertently injuring a portion of the Koran. This time, instead of the expected tit-bit, a dead night-adder was wrapped up and presented. When she unfolded the innermost paper, and the snake slipped out, with a horrid writhe, across her hand, Sarah quietly sank backwards and fainted away, her lips turning perfectly white. By dint of throwing water over her, chafing her hands, and bathing her lips with brandy, she was revived from her swoon, though not without some difficulty.

Sarah has now been for a long time the inmate of an

English country rectory, where, let us hope, no unfeeling jokes at her expense embitter her declining years.

Of a far less docile disposition than Sarah was a large baboon kept by T—— at the Diamond Fields. The incessant damage wrought by this creature among his master's property and that of neighbours, and the frequent doctors' bills of which he was the occasion, made him rather an expensive pet. He was kept chained up, but would now and then break loose, on which occasions he never failed to make an excellent use of his opportunities and enjoy as good a "time" as possible before Nemesis overtook him in the form of recapture and well-deserved chastisement.

One day, for instance, T——, on returning to his tent, was considerably surprised to find his bed occupied by Mr. Adonis, who, after getting into the shower-bath, pulling the string, and receiving the consequent ducking, had retired in a drenched and dripping condition to the blankets, within which he had comfortably ensconced himself, and from whence he gazed impudently at his master. He no doubt thought that he had well earned the luxuries of bath and bed by his busy morning's work among the contents of T——'s canvas house; and indeed that once cosy little abode now offered to the owner's eye a very good representation of chaos on a small scale. A bottle of acid, in which were a number of diamonds, had been thrown outside and the contents scattered in the sand; T——'s watch had been pulled to pieces and flung through the window; and altogether every conceivable piece of mischief had been done. On attempting to secure and tie up the offender, T—— received a severe bite through the leg; on which, naturally irate, he seized his gun, and capital punishment would then and there have been inflicted but for the discovery that the wily Adonis had balked retributive justice by carefully pulling every cartridge to pieces.

Among the numerous vices of this baboon was an incorrigible addiction to stimulants; and after indulging in his favourite drink—gin and ginger-beer—he might very profitably have been displayed on the platform of a temperance lecturer, as the Spartans exhibited their helots, in illustration of the evils of drunkenness. The manner in which, after a drop too much, he invariably persisted in walking upright was unpleasantly suggestive of drunken humanity; so too was his urgent need of soda-water to allay the parched condition of his mouth on the following morning. He would draw the cork with his strong teeth, holding the bottle close to his lips, and taking the greatest care to lose none of the refreshing gas.

He could throw stones with the unerring aim of a schoolboy; and, being of a revengeful disposition, and possessed of a wonderful memory, he never failed to requite any insult or injury received. Once a Zulu offended him by striking him with a stick. A long time passed, and then one day the man, who had quite forgotten all about it, came within reach of the baboon's tether, and—blissfully ignorant of the vengeful feelings lurking in the breast of the quadrumane—offered him something to eat. But Adonis, who had not forgotten, and who was only too glad to pay off old scores, caught the man by the hand, and, drawing him towards him, bit and punished him severely.

Here is another tale of revenge, in which the poor ape played but a passive part in the hands of the "superior" animal. A colonist, having killed a baboon, and owing several of his neighbours a long-standing grudge, bethought him of a truly fiendish manner of revenging himself. Though it is unlikely that he had ever read of Tantalus, he proceeded somewhat after that classical example, and, cutting up the baboon, made him into a stew, in which savoury disguise he served him up as the *pièce de résistance* at a dinner to which all the obnoxious neighbours were bidden. The dish proved a delicious one, and all the visitors ate of Pelops Cynocephalus with great relish. The tableau may be imagined when, at the end of the banquet, the host told his guests what they had eaten.

It must require considerable hardness of heart to kill a baboon; for the creature is so horribly and uncannily human-looking, and, when wounded, cries in a pathetic manner which must appeal to all but the most callous of consciences. A hunter once told T—— that he felt like a murderer after shooting one of them, and seeing how in its dying agonies it pressed one finger upon the hole made by the bullet; crying like a child as it fixed its eyes on him with piteous looks of reproach.

Although the miniature Zoo at Swaylands never boasted of a tame cynocephalus, we numbered among our feathered friends one of the gods of ancient Egypt in the shape of as tiny and chubby a little Horus as ever sat for his portrait to the sculptors of Philæ or Thebes. He was but a wee thing, about the size of a wild dove, but possessed an amount of intelligence which made him one of the most interesting even among Cape pets. Sad to say, the poor little fellow was minus one wing. T——, noticing him one day flying near the house, and not knowing what bird he was, brought him down with a small rifle bullet. The shot passed through the wing, so completely smashing it that the only thing we could do was to take it off close to the body. We tied it up at once and stopped the bleeding, the plucky little patient never uttering a sound, though his jewel-like eyes seemed really to blaze with anger. They were the most wonderful eyes imaginable, almost owl-like in size and roundness, and of a lovely red with an orange tinge. A ruby with a candle behind it is what I imagine would come nearest to them in colour. The plumage of Horus, instead of being speckled and barred with different shades of brown like that of the falcons one is accustomed to see, was of the loveliest silver-grey, darkest on the back and wing, and shading off gradually into very pale grey on the head, and into purest white on the breast and beneath the body; the breast feathers being soft and fluffy, like eider-down. The legs and feet were bright yellow, the bill dark grey, edged with yellow, and a circle of dark feathers round the eyes, drawn off into a long line at each side, gave a sphinx-like appearance to the wise-looking little head. Altogether, Horus was one of the most beautiful little birds we have seen. We took it for granted that he was the sacred falcon; and it will be a disappointment to us if, one day, some learned ornithologist tells us we were quite wrong.

The little fellow recovered rapidly; and, although on the first day after the amputation we had to put food down his throat, getting viciously punished by his needle-pointed bill and claws, on the second he took meat from our hands, eating voraciously as much as we would give him, and even coming after us for more; though, not having yet learned to steer himself under his altered circumstances, he hobbled in a very clumsy and crab-like fashion, now and then making futile efforts to fly, and tumbling down on his side. Soon, however, he learned to walk straight, and would follow us about like a little dog, with the quaintest short steps. He was soon tame and friendly with all but the meerkat, for which he showed great animosity, and on which he would jump spitefully—or perhaps hungrily?—whenever it came near him. Possibly, in a wild state, small animals of this kind were his natural prey. He did not object to Toto, who indeed—with the sole exception of his rival and arch-enemy Bobby—has never failed to get on well with all his heterogeneous companions.

Horus, debarred by his infirmity from active exercise, and condemned to a somewhat humdrum life, sought consolation in the pleasures of the table, and developed an enormous appetite. He shared the spoils of the mousetraps with Bobby, and would take raw and cooked meat from our hands with equal relish. Indeed I am afraid we overfed him, and induced apoplexy. At any rate, one evening as we sat reading after dinner, he dropped quietly from his perch, and died without a flutter.

The aasvogel, a repulsively ugly, bald-headed, bare-necked bird of the most pronounced vulture type, is very common in South Africa, especially in the regions where game is most plentiful. These denizens of the air seem to be perpetually hovering, on the watch for prey, at such immense heights as to be quite out of range of human vision; though their own keen sight enables them instantly to detect the prospect of a feed, and if an animal is killed, or even only wounded, they are at once aware of the fact, and, swooping down from their airy height, sail straight to the spot.

Perhaps you are a "new chum" out hunting, and you bring down an antelope. Although, at the moment of firing your shot, you would have been ready to take your affidavit that—

> "No birds were flying overhead,
> There were no birds to fly,"—

your game has hardly fallen before, far up in the grey-blue, a tiny speck appears, at first only just visible, but rapidly increasing in size; then another, and yet another floats into sight, "and still they come," till at last the heavens seem all alive with birds approaching from every direction, outlined against the cloudless sky in different degrees of size and clearness, according to perspective, but all making the straightest of bee-lines towards the wounded animal. In the Free State, where these birds are very numerous, T——, hunting on horseback, has sometimes found that before he could reach the spot where his antelope had fallen the aasvogels were already on it, and had commenced operations by plucking out the eyes, their special tit-bits.

These nastiest of birds think nothing of overeating themselves till their condition resembles that of Mark Twain's jumping frog after the famous dose of shot, and, when gorged after a good "square" meal, they are so heavy that they have to run a long way before they can rise into the air. On these occasions, if you are active and have a good long whip, you can catch them by switching the lash round their ugly, bare necks. But a little experience teaches you that this sport has its drawbacks, as the aasvogel invariably swarms with animal life of the most objectionable kind.

Owls are plentiful enough in the Karroo; so too are those other nocturnal birds, the goat-suckers, which at sundown begin to fly about, uttering their weird, plaintive cry. They are queer-looking birds, and seem all out of proportion, with a broad, short head and immensely wide bill, surrounded by stiff bristles like a cat's whiskers. On examining a specimen shot near our house, we were amused to find that, by looking into this preposterous bill, we could distinctly see the creature's eyes through the semi-transparent roof of the mouth.

Another of our feathered eccentricities, the butcher-bird, called by the colonists Jack Hanger, likes to eat his game high; and you often come across mimosa-bushes which, stuck all over with small birds, beetles, locusts, etc., impaled on the long, stiff thorns, form his well-stocked larder.

In such a land of snakes as South Africa it is necessary for the birds to resort to many clever and thoughtful devices for the protection of eggs and young; and some of the "homes without hands" are most ingeniously planned and exquisitely constructed.

The golden oriole hangs her graceful nest on the very furthest end of a long bough—over water, if possible, for extra safety,—and always gives the preference to the drooping branches of the willow. The nest is shaped just like a Florence flask with the end curved over; and it is next to impossible for a snake to penetrate into its interior.

Even prettier and more wonderfully made is the nest of the kapok bird, a little creature resembling a tom-tit. The material used in the construction of this small domicile is a kind of wild cotton, well named by the Boers *kapok* (snow). The nest, which is very compact, and looks as if it were made of soft, white felt, is of much the same shape as the oriole's brown flask; but near the outlet it is dented in, forming a kind of second or exterior nest, in which the little paterfamilias mounts guard over his household gods, effectually closing the aperture by the pressure of his back against the curving end of the tube above him. The white felt is very thick and firm throughout the globular part of the flask, but gradually diminishes in density along the neck, till at the orifice it is so thin and loosely woven that the soft edges, pressed together by the bird, remain interlaced even after he has flown from his sentry-box. No apparent aperture is left; and the little stronghold is quite impregnable, and ready to baffle the wiliest of ophidian marauders, until Mrs. Kapok, by flying out, re-opens the tunnel.

Snakes are indeed one of the greatest drawbacks to South African life. There are so many of them, they are of such deadly sorts, and the obtrusive familiarity and utter absence of ceremony with which they come into the houses render the nerves of newly-arrived inmates liable at any moment to receive a severe shock. After a time, of course, finding that every one you meet has some startling experiences to relate, of the discovery of intrusive snakes in all sorts of places where they were most unlooked-for and least desirable, you become somewhat inured to this unpleasant feature of colonial existence, and move about your house with the caution of one who would not be surprised to find a snake anywhere.

T——, dressing one morning during the early days of his Cape life, had just inserted his foot at one end of his trousers, when a night-adder—a most deadly little snake, with an evil habit of going about at hours when all respectable reptiles are in bed—dropped out at the other. One of our neighbours considerably damaged his drawing-room by firing several shots at a large cobra, which had startled his wife by paying an unwelcome call. Another friend, exploring the depths of her rather dark china-closet, put her hand on a snake, comfortably coiled up beside the teacups. And a ghastly tale we heard, of some one in bed, putting his hand under the pillow at night for his pocket-handkerchief, and pulling out a puff-adder, makes one feel that—for those at least who live at the Cape—there is more of common sense than of irony in Mark Twain's assertion that it is safest not to go to bed.

We were more fortunate than our neighbours, and never during our four years' residence did I find in any of our rooms that snake for which—as the old lady for the burglar—I was continually looking. Perhaps we owed our immunity to the narrow strips of horse-hair material, with the rough edge pointing upwards, which T——, having read somewhere that no snake will cross this prickly barrier, had nailed along the threshold of each outer door. In the store, which did not communicate with the house, and the door of which was fortified by no friendly spikes, we did occasionally kill a snake—attracted, no doubt, by the legions of fat mice which ran riot among the sacks. The fowl-house, too, would often be thrown into a state of wild excitement and frenzied cackling by the visits of these dreaded reptiles—most inveterate of egg-stealers.

One day, soon after we came up-country, Nancy suddenly burst in upon us, her red turban all awry, and her speech so incoherent with agitation that the only intelligible words were "Missis! *Turkey!!* Missis!

Snake!!!" On running out, we found the whole poultry-yard in commotion, and the hens clamouring as if each had laid at least a dozen eggs; while our nine turkeys stood drawn up in a row, pictures of imbecile consternation, chattering feebly as they, one and all, made a dead point at a little empty packing-case, protruding from behind which we could just see the ugly, broad head of a young puff-adder. The enemy was soon despatched; and while the turkeys recovered their equanimity—which process took a long time—I indulged in the pleasure so dear to any one with a taste for natural history, and took a thorough survey of this, the first good-sized puff-adder I had seen. And what a repulsive creature it was, with its short, thick, swollen-looking body, toad-like head, and utterly evil countenance! Only the hideous cerastes, with little demon-like horns—so common in North Africa—comes anywhere near a puff-adder in thorough-paced villany of expression.

Of all the Cape snakes the puff-adder is not only the deadliest, but by far the most to be feared. For, being of the same colour as the ground, it is extremely difficult to see: it is lazy, too, and will not take the trouble to get out of your way as every other snake does; yet, when roused, it is very active, and comes at you backwards, springing a long distance with accurate aim. If you are in front of it you are safe, as it cannot strike forward. One morning, T——, lifting up the rug in which he had been sleeping out on the veldt, found the flattened body of a puff-adder, which had evidently crept between the folds for warmth, and which he had unconsciously crushed to death.

Cobras, some of which are quite six feet in length, are very numerous in the Karroo. At certain seasons this snake is very aggressive, and will come at you boldly if you happen to be between it and its nest. T——, when out shooting one day with a pointer, suddenly saw a cobra lift itself up and strike the dog. The venom was so swift in its operation that the poor animal only turned round once, and died almost immediately.

The *schaapsticker*, which always reminded me of the beautiful but deadly coral-snakes of South America, has a wonderfully-marked skin, the pretty pattern and bright tints of which might well be utilized by some artistic designer of floor-cloths. A delicate, coral-like red predominates among the colours; and altogether the creature is so small and pretty that it is difficult to believe it is one of the most venomous of snakes. It is particularly destructive to cattle and sheep, hence its name, the literal translation of which is "sheep-stinger."

Some of the tree-snakes, too, are very beautiful; and, many of them being of the same bright green as the foliage, a close look is required to distinguish them as they lurk beneath it on the watch for birds, or for little mice which sometimes climb up into bushes, or into the lower branches of trees.

Lizards are very plentiful throughout the Karroo; and, as you walk through the veldt, hundreds of them, startled by your footsteps, dart away in all directions from one isolated tuft of bush to another, as if running for their little lives. In strong contrast to these bright, active creatures of the sunshine are the slow-moving, pallid-complexioned house-lizards which are so unpleasantly common. There are few things uglier than one of these *hikés*. With his flat, round toes, serving the purpose of suckers whereby he is enabled to retain his foothold as he perches, fly-like, on the ceilings, his low, criminal type of face, brightened by none of the quaint, antediluvian air of wisdom which redeems the chameleon's honest ugliness, and with his general unhealthy and uncanny appearance, it is no wonder that among the ignorant natives he has the reputation of being as venomous as he looks, and that from one end of the country to the other he is more dreaded than any snake. Yet it is somewhat puzzling to think how he can inflict a poisonous bite, when, on looking into his mouth, you perceive that he has no teeth.

An object of even more superstitious dread is that mysterious and deadly creature—half-quadruped, half-reptile, and certainly altogether fabulous—the so-called dassie-adder. Throughout the whole country you hear accounts of this strange animal from Boers, Kaffirs, and Hottentots; many of the coloured race declare that they have seen it, and, though some laugh at the tale, the belief in it is evidently very general. The anterior portion of the mythical creature's body is supposed to be that of a dassie, or rock-rabbit (the coney of Scripture), to which are joined, in somewhat mermaid-like fashion, the thick body and blunt tail of a snake resembling a puff-adder. According to all accounts the dassie-adder, whose bite is instantly fatal, is most vindictive, and, running with all the swiftness of a dassie, will chase any one who comes near it. Some say, too, that it goes about at night.

The dassies, so terrible in their fictitious semi-reptile state, are in real life very harmless, timid little animals. They are gregarious, and live among the rocks in such inaccessible places that it is most difficult to capture one of them; and a tame dassie is among the rarest of Karroo pets, so securely do these "feeble folk" make "their houses in the rocks." In appearance the dassie is very like a little brown guinea-pig; as regards intelligence, too, he is just about the equal of his rather uninteresting piebald cousins, and, although he is as pretty, soft-coated and gentle as you could wish, and in his mild, placid way gets very tame, he is nowhere in comparison with that prince of pets, a meerkat.

A not unlikely solution of the dassie-adder mystery seems to be that in all probability the puff-adders prey upon the little denizens of the rocks; and a large snake may occasionally have been seen with a half-swallowed dassie in his mouth, just as a common snake sometimes displays, protruding from his jaws, the head and forelegs of the inconveniently fat frog which he is unable to gulp down in a hurry. The negro mind is quite capable of evolving a fabulous animal out of even such slight grounds as this.

Of "creepy-crawlies" of all kinds the Karroo possesses more than enough, and—like the snakes—they invade the house, and make themselves at home in a manner which is free and easy rather than pleasant. Legions of venomous centipedes, scorpions, and big, bristly-legged spiders of the tarantula tribe lurk in the old reed ceilings; from whence they drop playfully down now and then, to the consternation of the unwary inmate sitting beneath, on whose head or book they chance to land. Or, if they do not drop down on you, they lie in wait about the room in well-chosen points of vantage, where their sudden discovery is sure to give you a horrid jump, even if you are lucky enough to get off without a venomous bite or sting.

One evening, as I was getting ready for bed—oblivious for once of cautious habits acquired, years before, in that land of "jiggers," the West Indies, where you never venture to walk slipperless, even across your bedroom—my bare foot suddenly encountered what seemed like the point of a red-hot needle sticking straight up out of the floor; and, looking down, I found that I had trodden on a scorpion. Fortunately, it was not one of the large black ones, which are the most venomous, but only a light-coloured specimen, about two inches and a half in length. It was, however, quite bad enough; and although T—— recklessly poured away over the foot our whole photographic supply of ammonia, and made me drink the greater part of a bottle of strong Cape wine in the hope of neutralizing the poison—though, alas! only producing other and sad results—it was many hours before that red-hot needle showed any signs of cooling down. And then an exaggerated form of "pins and needles" set in, followed by what resembled a succession of powerful electric shocks running up the leg at intervals of two or three minutes. Altogether, the victim of a scorpion's sting can well realize the feelings of gouty patients, who dread to see even their best friends coming within five or six yards of them. It was two days before I could put my foot to the ground; and then, for several more, I could only hobble painfully with the aid of a stick.

Colonial boys are fond of setting scorpions to fight with tarantulas. The great spiders are most pugnacious, and seem only too glad of an opportunity to fight with anything. T—— once watched one of them in desperate battle with a centipede. The vicious spider, whose body was as large as that of a mouse, seized his antagonist and shook him savagely, just as a terrier shakes a rat; then, letting him go for a time, he would spring upon him, pick him up, and worry him again, apparently with fiendish pleasure. He continued this mode of warfare until the final collapse of the poor centipede, whose pluck in facing such an adversary at all deserves to be commended.

Prominent among insect nuisances are ants of many different sorts and sizes, the worst of all being the mischievous rice ants. Many a carpet or curtain is utterly ruined by these creatures, which have a trick of coming up unexpectedly through the floor in large numbers, generally during the night, when they can carry on their destructive work without interruption.

They work with a zeal worthy of a better cause, and the amount of damage their powerful jaws can do in one night is almost incredible.

Very pretty necklaces are made of the threaded eggs of one kind of ant. They are rough and irregular in shape, and possess such a soft lustre, that—but for their deep golden colour—they might almost be taken for inferior pearls.

It is some satisfaction to know that the ranks of Cape ants are considerably thinned by several inveterate enemies. One of these is that strange burrowing animal the ant-bear, called by the Dutch *aardvaark* (earth-pig).* There is one in the Zoo; and it is about as uncanny and nightmare-like a beast as could be imagined or dreamed of—a sort of crazy combination of calf and pig, reminding one of the Mock Turtle in "Alice's Adventures." Like that tearful animal, it possesses a head and body which do not in the smallest degree appear to belong to each other. The longest, narrowest and boniest of calves' heads, so pallid and sickly in complexion, and so entirely hairless, as to appear not only dead, but neatly scraped and cleaned all ready for cooking, is joined—without the intervention of any neck to speak of—to a fat, pig-like body, very scantily clothed with short, bristly hairs. The eyes are large and dark, the bare, pink ears are of rabbit-like proportions, and the calf's head terminates in a pig's snout, thickly lined with hair. This latter is the only hirsute adornment possessed by the goblin-like coun-

* *Orycteropus capensis.*

tenance, to which a very cynical expression is given by the animal's ugly trick of wrinkling up its enormously long snout. The thick legs, and the feet, armed with large claws, are immensely strong; so, too, is the broad, flat, almost hairless tail, about the shape of which there is something unpleasantly suggestive of a puff-adder. The specimen in the Zoo has a damaged tail, the result of the force the captors found it necessary to use in dragging it from its hole. A riem was once tied to the tail of an ant-bear, and a span of oxen fastened on to draw it out of the ground. But, after much ineffectual tugging, the experiment ended in the breaking of the riem—or of the tail—our informant had forgotten which; at any rate the animal remained in its hole.

Many a time does the unwary rider, cantering across the veldt, come to sudden grief in one of the deep, trap-like holes made by the ant-bear, which seems by no means an uncommon animal. But it is quite possible to live many years in South Africa, and, however often you may tumble into its holes, never once see the creature itself. For, being of nocturnal habits, it is active only at night, when it tunnels its way underground like a mole, occasionally coming to the surface, and now and then emerging in very unexpected places.

Some members of a hunting-party, camping out for the night, were much surprised to see the ground heave up suddenly in the centre of their tent, the passing of an ant-bear a little below the surface being the cause of the miniature earthquake. And during the war in

Zululand an Irish sentry was on guard at midnight, when suddenly, close to him, the ground opened, and out of it rose a ghastly living Jack-in-the-box. The moonbeams shone full on the horrid form, long head, and deadly-pale, calf-like face; and the man—small blame to him—dropped his gun, deserted his post, and fled in horror, shouting to his astonished comrades the awful news that he had seen Old Nick himself! And indeed, if, on one of our moonlight strolls about the farm, an ant-bear had suddenly risen in our path, I am quite sure that we should have taken to our heels with equal alacrity.

The cage of the Cape ant-bear at the Zoo being next to that of the American ant-eater, a good opportunity is afforded for observing the marked dissimilarity of the two animals, which indeed could hardly be more unlike each other. One of the numerous points in which they differ is that the American ant-eater is toothless, while the *aardvaark* possesses teeth.

The ant-lion, so often pictured in books of natural history, is common in the Karroo; and it was a great pleasure for us when, for the first time, we saw him in real life, and examined his cleverly-constructed, funnel-shaped trap, hollowed out in the soft, sliding sand,—down which his victims tumble, to find him waiting open-mouthed at the bottom.

Talking of the ant-lion reminds one of another excavator, still more familiar to Cape colonists, the trap-door spider. His "diggings" are in the form of a perpendicular, cylinder-shaped box, the lid of which, level with the surface of the ground, is so neatly made that it is quite impossible to detect it when closed.

The walking-leaf tribe is very largely represented in South Africa; and besides simulating leaves of many different kinds, the creatures assume numerous other forms, some looking just like pieces of dried stick, others like bits of straw, blades of grass, etc. The plant, or portion of a plant, which they personate so admirably, is always the chosen resting-place on which they sit, motionless and meditative, often defying detection. The praying mantis is worshipped by the Hottentots, who perhaps, like the ancient Greeks and Romans, look on him as a kind of soothsayer or fortune-teller ($\mu\acute{a}\nu\tau\iota\varsigma$). But in spite of being the Hottentot god, and of possessing such a pious-sounding scientific name as *Mantis religiosa*, he is a most pugnacious little beast; and if he has a difficulty to settle with one of his brethren, the pair will fight it out like the Kilkenny cats.

Not long ago, at a North African picnic, one of these same little creatures caused much amusement by the tact which he displayed in doing just the right thing at the right time, and in the prettiest manner. It was a very hot day, so close and oppressive that we all felt rather languid; and conversation flagged as we sat at luncheon round the table-cloth spread on the ground in the interior of a large tent. Suddenly, during a long pause, a little mantis appeared on the scene. With a jaunty air, and with all the cool self-possession of a popular performer advancing, confident of success, towards the footlights, he stepped on to the tablecloth, and, crossing it in a bee-line, drew up before Her Britannic Majesty's Consul, to whom, with many jerky inclinations of his gaunt, bright-green body, he made what appeared to be a series of most obsequious bows. Then, having obeyed the first requirements of etiquette, he passed slowly along the line of guests, halting occasionally and paying his respects to one or the other. He seemed quite unabashed by all the notice and applause which he received; and as the plate in which he finally deposited himself was handed round among the guests, he calmly surveyed each one in turn, while continuing, very literally, to "bow and scrape." If he had been a paid performer, engaged beforehand, he could not have played his little part better; and all agreed in giving him a vote of thanks for his timely appearance, which just gave us the mental pick-me-up which, on that enervating day, we all needed. I believe some one carried him home at last in a paper cage; though whether he fulfilled the brilliant promise of his first introduction to human society, and became an intelligent pet, we never heard.

CHAPTER XIII.

OUR NEIGHBOURS.

Hospitality of Cape colonists—Cheating and jealousy in business—Comfortless homes—Spoilt children—Education—The "Schoolmaster"—Convent schools—A priest-ridden nation—The *Nachtmaal*—Old French names—A South African duke in Paris—Fine-looking men—Fat women—Ignorance of *Vrouws*—Boers unfriendly to English—A mean man.

THERE is much to be admired in the character of those decidedly unpolished diamonds, the colonial-born, English-speaking inhabitants of the Karroo. They are a fine, sturdy, self-reliant race, splendidly fitted in every way for their extremely rough-and-ready surroundings. In kindliness and hospitality they are unsurpassed, even by the much-praised dwellers in Arab tents or white, flat-roofed Moorish houses; and in the isolated homesteads where they live their rough, but simple and healthy lives, the heartiest reception is invariably accorded alike to friends, slight acquaintances, and even perfect strangers. Perhaps you are one of the latter, and, on a long journey, you outspan at the dam of a farm, with the intention of remaining only long enough to give the horses the necessary water and rest before you *trek* again. But no sooner is your cart or spider seen to stop than you are sought out, with kind and pressing invitation to come in. No matter how full the house may already be, how late or inconvenient the hour of your unexpected arrival on a Cape farm, a place is always found for you at the table; and, if needed, some sort of a night's lodging, of however *impromptu* a description, will be prepared for you. The colonist joyfully makes you welcome to his best. If you are staying in his house, a mount or a seat in his conveyance is always at your disposal; and the longer you can remain, the better he and all his kind-hearted family are pleased. It is true that their home is far from being a luxurious one, and that none of them have much idea of comfort; but the latter article being, on account of the isolation and of the bad servants, somewhat difficult of attainment, it is on the whole just as well that no one misses it sufficiently to regret its absence; and one cannot but admire and envy the philosophical manner in which the colonists take things as they come, making themselves perfectly happy under any circumstances.

Altogether there is so much that is lovable in the colonial character, that you are sometimes disappointed to find that there is a reverse to this bright side of the picture, and that—even by those who have received you the most hospitably, and who apparently, while you were their guest, could not do enough for you—you are liable, in business transactions, to be woefully cheated. It is thought no disgrace to get the better of any one in a bargain, whether on an iniquitously large or contemptibly small scale; on the contrary, it is considered rather clever and smart to "do a shot" on the guileless and unsuspecting new chum, fresh from a country where a somewhat different code of honour obtains.

Business jealousies, too, are another source of trouble to the uninitiated. If any farmer has a project which seems likely to turn out a good thing for him, he had better be careful that no bird of the air whispers it about beforehand among his neighbours and rivals, who, one and all, will only be too glad if they can bring his plans to naught.

Time seems to be of no more value to the Cape colonists than it is to the followers of Islam, and "letting things slide" is pretty generally the order of the day. One is rather puzzled at this weak point in otherwise active, energetic characters; and certainly, living as these people do in the splendid air of the Cape—exhilarating as champagne, and making all who inhale it feel glad to be alive—they cannot, like the limp, supine inhabitants of Eastern lands, plead the excuse of an enervating climate. Much of the discomfort in the houses is due to this frightful habit of procrastinating. Whatever is broken is, as often as not, left unmended for an indefinite time; little repairs, which need but the minimum of time and trouble, but the neglect of which would cause daily annoyance and discomfort to any but these easy-going mortals, are put off from week to week and from month to month. And every one is just as happy and contented, with violent draughts and clouds of dust blowing in through two or three broken windows at once; or with a glass outer door whose handle has been off for months, and which continually flaps noisily backwards and forwards, admitting gusts of cold wind and flocks of turkeys and fowls into the room; as if all things were in perfect order. Poultry and domestic animals, indeed, have it all their own way on Karroo farms with the delightful freedom enjoyed by their brethren in Irish cabins. At one house, for instance, if the dining-room was left for a moment when the cloth was laid for a meal, half a dozen fowls would be on the table, picking the bread to pieces; while in another I have several times assisted our hosts in ejecting a too-friendly pig from the bedroom. To give South African pigs their due, I must say that in that driest of climates they are less uncleanly in their persons, and hence rather less objectionable indoors, than they would be in Europe. But we had English prejudices, and discountenanced the visits of members of the farm-yard; and Toto had standing orders, which he faithfully obeyed, to keep the rooms clear of live stock of all kinds, with the exception of privileged pets.

Even more terrible than the intrusive animals are the spoilt children. During their earlier years the little colonists are left very much to themselves: they run wild, like young colts, about their native farm, no one takes the trouble to interfere with them, and they are allowed to retain, unchecked, all the rude, rough habits which they have acquired from their uncivilized Hottentot nurse-girls. They do as they like, say whatever comes uppermost, and behave at table in any sort of outrageous fashion that pleases them; while the father and mother sit unmoved, apparently surprised at nothing their progeny may see fit to do. The latter being totally unencumbered by bashfulness, the presence of strangers acts as no restraint; and a dinner taken in the company of a large family of boys, of stolid parents, and indifferent elder sisters, is for the newly-imported English visitor a novel and rather startling experience, the details of which, however, are best left to oblivion.

But, on the whole, the young Africander's bringing-up — unpleasant though he certainly is during the process — is no doubt the best possible one to fit him for the rough and active life of the farms, and to form in him that independent character and those habits of self-reliance and smartness in money matters which, when he is grown up, stand him in such good stead. And he *does* grow up with astounding rapidity; being at fifteen a thorough man of business, able to "do a deal" with any one, and taking good care, you may be sure, that the transaction is no unprofitable one to himself. In this respect he affords a decided contrast to the average young Englishman, who, at twenty-five, is often — where business matters are concerned — as inexperienced as a boy.

The difficulties in the way of providing the children with a good education are by no means one of the least of South African drawbacks; especially for those living on the far-off country farms. Colonial schools do not seem to be much in favour, at least for boys, and the great ambition of a Cape parent is to send his sons home to be educated in Europe—most frequently for the medical profession, a doctor's position being the most coveted one in the colony. In the Edinburgh University, especially, the Africander element is in great force. Those parents who cannot afford to have their boys educated in Europe generally contrive to secure the services of some broken-down gentleman, occasionally even of a clergyman, who lives on the farm and—too often for a shamefully small salary, indeed in one or two instances for nothing but his keep—fills the post of tutor, or, as his employers call him, "schoolmaster," to the turbulent young tribe. As may be imagined, his life is not a very enviable one, the breaking-in process being all the harder in consequence of the long period, prior to his advent, when his charges were allowed to run wild out of doors all day long—to the immense benefit, no doubt, of their robust young bodies, but to the utter neglect of all intellectual and moral training.

The schoolmaster does not seem to have been a very general institution in the days when some of the older colonists were young; and a business correspondence with Karroo farmers sometimes elicits the wildest vagaries of orthography. T——, for instance, received a letter from one of our neighbours, in which the following sentences occurred: "Your hostridges are vary onpleasand on the public outspan. Pleas to try and halter tham." Another correspondent, intent on the purchase of ostriches, told us he wished "to bye buirds."

For girls, the convent schools in several of the larger towns are undoubtedly the best, both as regards the good, sensible education imparted, and the refined, ladylike manners which are invariably acquired by all who have been brought up under the tutelage of the nuns. Throughout the whole country, the convent-bred girls can always be recognised at a glance, and the contrast is very striking between them and the less fortunate ones who possess but the superficial education and second-rate manners of the average colonial boarding-school. Even the daughters of the roughest Boers, if sent to a convent school, are turned out perfect ladies, and return to their up-country homes with gentle and gracious manners strangely out of keeping with their uncouth surroundings. But there are many parents, of course, to whom all the advantages of convent education could not compensate for that insuperable objection, the risk of Romanizing influence; and intending settlers in the colony who do not wish to expose their daughters to that risk will do well to bring out a good governess with them, and keep the girls at home.

The Boer's great desire, like that of his English-speaking neighbour, is to get his boys educated in Europe; but, instead of the medical profession, the pastorate is the object of his ambition. For these Cape Dutch, although Protestants, are quite as priest-ridden as any Roman Catholic nation; the *predikant* is a great man indeed throughout the widespread circle of his parishioners, and to offend him, or even to fail in paying him the exact amount of deference he considers his due, means to be boycotted.

The *nachtmaal*, or communion, is only administered— as among Scotch Presbyterians—twice or three times during the year; and on these rare occasions the little town or village where there is a Dutch church becomes the lively scene of an immense gathering of Boers, *vrouws*, and families. They have come, many of them from long distances of three or four days' journey, plodding along in waggons drawn by long spans of oxen, driving in roomy conveyances of every possible queer and antiquated shape, or travelling on horseback— the stout, ungainly women, in their white *kappjes* and gaudily-coloured dresses, cantering clumsily by the side of their lords. The crowd of outspanned vehicles, drawn up close together, form a kind of large camp; and, the Boer being always ready to combine piety with business—and, if need be, with a good deal of cheating, —the *nachtmaal* ends with a busy fair or market, in which a very brisk trade is carried on, all kinds of farm produce being sold or bartered.

In nearly all the Dutch houses you find curious old family Bibles, many of them in black-letter, with quaint and interesting maps. In some of the latter, representing Africa, the lakes Victoria and Albert Nyanza are marked, though quite in the wrong places. The good old French names borne by so many of the Boers tell of their Huguenot descent; Du Plessis, De Villiers, Du Toit, Du Barry, etc., are all names of frequent occurrence in South Africa, although the French language is never spoken, the Dutch having prohibited its use among the refugees when the latter settled in the colony. Some time ago, Napoleon III., anxious to restore the ancient nobility, sent for one of these Boers, who, in the old country, was the heir to a dukedom, inviting him to resume his title and estates. The colonist came to Paris, and, after giving European life a fair trial, became homesick for his vineyard and his farm, and—perhaps impelled by that attraction which seems to draw back to the Cape those who have once lived under its bright sky—decided in favour of his old-fashioned life, and, resigning all his ancestral rights, went joyfully home to the rough surroundings of his childhood.

Although the Boers are fine, well-built, handsome men, their feminine relatives, far from equalling them in good looks, are as fat and ungraceful as any inmates of Turkish harems. Fortunately, however, excessive obesity is in the eyes of a Boer the very quality of all others which constitutes the chief attraction of a *mooie vrouw* (handsome woman); and when he uses the latter expression you may be sure that he speaks of a ponderous being, no less than thirteen or fourteen stone in weight. In this matter of taste the Boers resemble not only the Turks, but also the Zulus, who can pay a woman no higher compliment than to compare her to a she-elephant. The *vrouws* become *passées* at a very early age, and are apparently shortlived in comparison with their lords, if one may judge from the fact that it is no uncommon thing to meet a man of fifty who has already had three wives.

Intellectually, no less than physically, the Boer

women are considerably the inferiors of the men. They have evidently lived for generations in blissful ignorance, with no more education than falls to the lot of the Oriental ladies they so closely resemble in figure. Their husbands and fathers have been quite contented with the existing state of things; and it is only of late years that a few of the more enlightened parents, beginning at last to recognise the value of female education, have been sending their daughters to the convent schools.

In Spain, an equally strong contrast may be observed between the men and the women; but it is reversed, the advantage being on the side of the *señoras*, who somehow appear too handsome and intelligent to belong to the ignoble, mean-looking men.

The Boers used to be very friendly with the English; but now—thanks to the sad and too well-known manner in which our Government has muddled South African affairs—we are most unpopular. Formerly, if an Englishman on his journey came to a Dutchman's house, he was most hospitably received—though etiquette demanded that on his departure he should offer money in payment for his food and bed, in order that his host might have the pleasure of refusing it; but now, were he to present himself, the chances are that the Boer would insultingly offer him a night's lodging in the negroes' quarters, as was once the case with T——.

Meanness is a prominent trait in the Boer's character. Indeed, the reputation which he has acquired

—not altogether justly—for being such a splendid shot, really and truly proceeds from his excessive care to make sure of his game, and thus waste no cartridges. Here is an instance which almost equals Max Adeler's mean man. When T——was at the Kimberley Diamond Fields, a Kaffir fell one day from the narrow pathway left between the claims into one of the latter, belonging to a Dutchman. He landed on the little table used by the Boer for sorting his diamonds, and—the height from which he had fallen being eighty feet—not only the table, but nearly every bone in the unfortunate man's body was broken. He seems, however, to have possessed a wonderfully strong constitution, and actually recovered from his terrible injuries; and, his case exciting very general sympathy among the kindly diamond-diggers, a subscription was made for him. But, long before he was convalescent, the Boer called on him, demanding payment for the broken table, the whole value of which did not amount to more than thirty shillings.

CHAPTER XIV.

GOOD-BYE.

Recalled to England—Regrets and farewells—Cape horses lacking in intelligence—"Old Martin"—A chapter of accidents—A horse "after Velasquez"—The Spy's revenge—Virtues and faults of Cape horses—Horse-sickness—Good-bye to Swaylands—Kaffir crane—The voyage home—Dogs in durance—St. Helena—A visit to Longwood—Home again.

AT last, after several busy and most enjoyable years of ostrich-farming life, the time came when—our presence being required in England—we bade farewell to our colonial home, and, leaving the management of affairs in the able hands of a friend from the old country, with whom T—— had recently entered into partnership, took our departure from Swaylands, not without many regrets. Although, within the wide circle enclosed by our wire fence, we were not leaving many of our human fellow-creatures, there were plenty of good-byes to be said; for those who live on these out-of-the-way farms come to be on very intimate and familiar terms with their live stock, and all our creatures—even the fowls, and those tamer members of our large family of ostriches which for years had been daily looking inquiringly in at our windows, and picking and stealing round the kitchen door—were old friends, from whom we were sorry to part.

But, strange to say, the very animal which in England becomes one of the friendliest seems here the least domesticated; and it cost us less of a pang to bid adieu to our horses than might be imagined by people at home, unacquainted with the surprising lack of intelligence which, in the Cape Colony, distinguishes the equine race. Their independent lives, and the freedom which most of them enjoy to roam as they will about the veldt, unfettered by the restraints of a stable, seem to have rendered them very indifferent to human society. It is no use trying to make a friend of your horse; he contemptuously repels all your advances, obstinately refuses to eat out of your hand, despises pieces of bread, lumps of sugar, and all such delicate little attentions wherewith you have never failed to win the heart of his English brother, and, however many years he may have lived with you, persists to the last in remaining on the coldest and most distant of terms.

Among all our horses the only really intelligent animal was one of Arab descent. But our good-bye to him was said a year before; and now, on leaving Swaylands, we can but take our last look at "the place where the old horse died." The faithful old grey friend who lies under that rough clump of bush was a favourite of long standing. He had belonged to T—— many years ago, was sold by him on leaving the colony, and, after changing hands several times, chiefly among acquaintances of his former owner—in remembrance of whom he acquired the name of "Old Martin"—was repurchased by T—— soon after we came out. Although by this time he was a long way past his prime, he was still considerably the best of all our horses, and for pluck and endurance we have never seen his equal. At the end of the longest day's journey—even though it had covered sixty miles—he would come in pulling as hard as at the start, and apparently as fresh. No matter how poor his condition—and South African horses do indeed get poor during long droughts—he was at all times equally ready for work. We never insulted him by carrying so unnecessary an article as a whip; for he did everything with a will, and whether cantering, trotting, or only walking, always seemed to be endeavouring to run away with you. As a lady's horse he was simply perfect, all his paces being equally delightful for the rider.

In former times T—— and his four-footed namesake had gone through many adventures together; and now, when after the lapse of years these two friends and comrades met again, the old horse instantly recognised his master with unmistakeable signs of pleasure.

One of these early adventures came very near costing the good grey his life. T——, during a journey on horseback, came one evening to a river crossed by an open railway-bridge consisting only of iron girders. To save time and avoid a circuitous route he decided to take a somewhat reckless short cut and lead the horse over that bridge. In this Blondin-like fashion they had proceeded about half-way across, when poor old Martin's foot slipped, and down he came, falling in such a position that his body lay prone on the narrow iron pathway formed by the rail and girder, while on either side two of his legs dangled helplessly over space. Sundown was approaching; so too was a train which, as T—— remembered, was very nearly due; but, though he tried his utmost to help the poor animal to his feet, all was unavailing, and presently the train hove in sight. T——, waving his handkerchief with wild gestures, succeeded in attracting the attention of the engine-driver, who stopped the train and came to his assistance. But, with all their efforts, they could not succeed in raising the horse from his perilous position; the train could wait no longer, and they had no choice but to resort to the kill-or-cure expedient of rolling him over into the water below. Falling from a height of some twenty-five feet, he went so deep into the mud at the bottom of the shallow African river that T—— was unable to pull him out, and had to leave him there all night. On coming back next morning with a span of oxen and some stout riems, he was horrified to find that during the night the unfortunate animal had sunk deeper and deeper into the mud, till little more than his nose remained above water. It was the work of much time and exertion to drag him out; and during the process his neck got such a twist that for the remainder of his days there was a crook in it, which caused his head to hang meditatively a little on one side.

Another time he was attacked by a large swarm of vicious bees, which settled all over him, stinging him so severely that his whole body swelled up, and he assumed the proportions of that preposterously inflated horse by Velasquez in the picture-gallery at Madrid. For three days the poor old fellow stood immoveable; then, after taking an enormous drink of water, he gradually recovered.

Very different, too, from the unintelligent Cape horses was "The Spy," a well-known steeple-chaser, imported into the colony by T—— some years ago. An incident which occurred during his voyage out recalls the oft-told anecdote of the elephant and the tailor. The horse-box in which the Spy was placed being just outside the door of the saloon, his head was in close proximity to the waiters as they passed and repassed during their attendance at meals. One of these waiters, being of a malicious turn of mind, found great enjoyment in teasing the unoffending animal, and missed no opportunity of giving him a rough knock on the nose in passing. For a while the Spy bore this treatment patiently; but he was biding his time, and at last had his revenge. One day, as the obnoxious waiter, bearing in either hand a steaming dish of currie and rice, was stepping briskly along to the saloon, he suddenly found himself grasped in a pair of powerful jaws, whisked clean off his legs, shaken like a rat in the grip of a terrier, and, finally, ignominiously dropped on to the deck among the *débris* and scattered contents of his dishes.

Although the horses produced by the Cape Colony are the best in South Africa, they have been much over-rated. It is true that a large number of them are capable of getting through a good deal of slow, continuous work under the saddle, with poor food and hardships as to shelter; but the vast majority of the colonial horses are in all respects indifferent animals, and devoid of good looks. In one point, perhaps, they surpass all other equine races in the world—their feet being generally excellent, and the hoofs so firm and hard as rarely to require shoeing, even on very long journeys. Many horses of most unprepossessing exterior are scarcely to be matched for speed and endurance in the field; but, taken *en masse*, South African horses are a failure. They are almost invariably poor and timid jumpers, and, when in harness, move but very small weights. A light cart containing two persons is sufficient to tax the powers of a pair of average horses, and even then jibbing is always imminent. At least eighty per cent. of the Cape horses are desperate stumblers, and uneasy in their paces—faults attributable to round, heavy shoulders and defective hind-quarters. Among the good horses the greater proportion are ill-tempered, and delight in buck-jumping, whenever they have the rare chance of being in good condition.

The terrible distemper known as "horse sickness" periodically causes great destruction in many parts of the colony; and the fear of it operates as a check on breeders, who would otherwise import better horses to improve their studs. A "salted horse"—one which has had horse-sickness—is very valuable, even if abounding in all kinds of equine misfortunes or faults. Such animals range in price from £25 to £100, according to age and quality. Horse-sickness is most partial in its operations; and sometimes, in the case of two adjoining farms, one will be severely attacked by the disease, while the other remains perfectly free from it.

And now, at length, the day of departure has come; and we leave Swaylands, though not in our own cosy little American spider. That fairy chariot, alas! is *hors de combat;* its strong, though delicate-looking wheels have succumbed at last to the roughness of Karroo roads and the dryness of the South African climate; and as we pass out at the little gate we take our last look at it as it lies there on the ground, a forlorn, sledge-like thing. What glorious drives we have had in that once daintiest and prettiest of little carriages—travelling to hunts or dances, fetching our mail, or sending off precious freights of feathers to the Port Elizabeth market! and how vividly the recollection of them comes back to us as we pass for the last time along the familiar Mount Stewart road!

Even now, at this time and distance, we can still conjure them up, and see and hear once more the well-known and loved sights and sounds of the Karroo. Animal and bird life start into quick motion all round us: the little *duyker* antelopes spring up from their forms among the bush, and dart gracefully away; the flights of pretty Namaqua partridges run along the ground quite close to us; the *knorhaans,* rending the air with discordant, over-powering noise, chatter out their loud disapproval of our approach; the little bright-eyed meerkats stare audaciously at us, then dive into their holes in pretended fear of us; the air is all full of the sweet scent of mimosa-blossoms, and T——, singing joyously in the overflow of good spirits induced by its pure, fresh, exhilarating qualities, enlivens the journey with one song after another as we spin merrily along on our airy, bicycle-like wheels; while Toto, equally happy, careers at our side, chasing every animal and bird that he sees, though seldom able to catch anything much swifter on its feet than a tortoise.

These tortoises, by the way, always afforded Toto excellent sport; he considered it his bounden duty to bring to us—no matter from what distance—all that he could possibly grasp with his teeth; and, many of them being much too large to be carried in this way, he was often obliged to put them down for a while, to rest his poor aching jaws. Sometimes he would come to a standstill before a gigantic specimen, and call us, with loud, excited barks, to the spot where some fifty pounds of splendid material for soup were to be had for the picking-up. He would stand barking triumphantly at the creature, which, in response, kept up a low, roaring noise, expressive of deepest disgust at his proceedings. And when the prize was secured, and we drove off with it safely ensconced at our feet, Toto was a proud dog indeed.

Somehow, on this last drive into Mount Stewart,

everything is tantalizingly looking its very best; the *veldt*, refreshed by recent rains, is of a lovely soft green, and delicate flowers peep from it in all directions; the dazzling sunshine—so soon to be exchanged for cold northern skies—seems brighter than ever; and, in the clear atmosphere of the Karroo, the bold outlines of the far-off Cock's Comb are lifted up, as it were, by a strange effect of mirage—the mountain appearing quite detached from the horizon, and with blue water flowing at its foot. Just before we reach the turn in the road which hides the homestead of Swaylands from our view, we stop and look back; and, if it must be owned, that last look at the poor little ugly house—our dear home for the past few years—is taken by not quite undimmed eyes.

Then on, at a brisk pace, to Mount Stewart, where, at the pleasant little hotel in which we have so often been hospitably entertained, the host and his numerous family are assembled in full force to bid us God-speed. I take my last, wistful look at a long-coveted tame Kaffir crane, a delightful bird, who, in his neat suit of softest French-grey plumage, stalks solemnly—as he has been doing any time these four or five years—about the precincts of station and hotel; and am introduced to a newly-captured baby jackal, which T——has just bought, and which is to accompany us to England. Then the train, at its usual leisurely pace, crawls down with us to Port Elizabeth. More good-byes—and at last we and all our zoological collection are safe on board the Union Company's *S.S. Mexican*;

T

and soon the coast of Algoa Bay recedes from our view.

Toto does not enjoy his journey as he did when outward-bound; for there are too many of the canine race on board, and one little pair of pugs in particular—belonging to richly-jewelled passengers of the Hebrew persuasion, who have not trained up their dogs in the way they should go—commence the voyage by invading everybody's cabin, and making themselves generally so objectionable that on the second day the captain's fiat goes forth for the impartial consignment of all the dogs—good, bad and indifferent—to hencoops. There they are accordingly, on the second-class deck, ranged in a dismal row, at one end of which poor little caged Anubis, the jackal-cub, yelps piteously for mother, brethren and freedom; and there, for the four weeks of the voyage, they are condemned to remain. All are profoundly miserable; but poor old Toto—being so much the largest—is the most to be pitied. In that narrow cage, where there is hardly room for him to turn round, he travels through the steaming heat of the tropics; his legs become cramped and stiff from want of exercise; he fattens like a Strasburg goose on the Irish stew and other substantial viands from the saloon table with which the waiters—cruelly generous—persist in stuffing him; and when, as a rare treat, he is allowed half an hour's liberty for what is ironically called a "run" on deck, he is able to do little more than sit down and pant.

With better luck than often falls to the lot of travellers by steamer, we remain a sufficient time at St. Helena to allow of a somewhat hurried visit to Longwood; and, going ashore with a good number of fellow-passengers, we charter the few carriages and saddle-horses to be had in the little town, and proceed, as fast as we can, up the steep, zigzag road. We notice that in this island there seem to be two completely different climates within a very short distance of one another. Down near the sea-level, bananas and other tropical plants grow luxuriantly in the close, stifling heat: but as we ascend we come into another climate; the air is almost cold, there is a fine, drizzling rain; blackberries, bracken, and other home-like plants border the roadside, and we might imagine ourselves in England, but for the bright-hued little birds which peep fearlessly at us from the bushes. Though the excursion is a most enjoyable one, especially after being cooped up on board ship, Longwood itself is disappointing, the house being quite dismantled, and containing nothing but a very beautiful bust of Napoleon, which has been placed by his family in one of the rooms.

Our passage is throughout a calm and prosperous one: we have pleasant company on board; there are none of the cliques and small enmities which so often spoil the enjoyment of a voyage; some of the passengers play and sing well; good concerts and theatricals enliven many of our evenings; and our only disappointment is the unkind fate which again brings us through Madeira in the dark. And at last, one lovely April morning—which seems to have been made on purpose to welcome returning colonists, spoilt by a long continuance of Cape sunshine—we drop quietly into Southampton; English violets and primroses are brought on board in delicious profusion; the usual hurried farewells are exchanged while most of us struggle wildly with refractory bags and wraps; Toto, in an alarmingly plethoric condition, waddles forth from his hen-coop; and very soon we are on *terra firma*, and—paying the first dread penalty of the newly-landed—pass through the ordeal of the Custom House. This turns out to be a very lengthy and tedious business; for, since we have been away, new and stringent regulations have come into force, and we find that our innocent cabin-trunks and hand-bags are all suspected of containing dynamite. Not until every package has been thoroughly ransacked are we allowed to depart, and seek our train. Then the latter bears us along through woodland scenery, brilliant with all the fresh tints of an English spring, which for us seems to have a new beauty. And in a few hours we find ourselves back in old, familiar scenes; friends from whom we have long been parted are round us once more; and the dear, delightful, rough South African life is a thing of the past.

www.ingramcontent.com/pod-product-compliance
Lightning Source LLC
Chambersburg PA
CBHW021955220426
43663CB00007B/824